ATTP 3-21.50

Infantry Small-Unit Mountain Operations

February 2011

I0026818

Headquarters, Department of the Army

Published by Books Express Publishing
Books Express Publishing, 2011
ISBN 978-1-78039-958-4

Books Express publications are available from all good retail and online booksellers. For
publishing proposals and direct ordering please contact us at: info@books-express.com

Army Tactics Techniques Procedures
No. 3-21.50

Headquarters
Department of the Army
Washington, DC, 28 February 2011

Infantry Small-Unit Mountain Operations

Contents

Preface

ATTP 3-21.50 provides perspective on Infantry company missions in an operational environment characterized by high-altitudes, rapidly changing climatic conditions, and rugged terrain. It also provides the small-unit leader with guidance on how company-sized units and below can conduct these operations. The mountain environment challenges all warfighting functions. Infantry units are full spectrum organizations, not specifically designed for mountain terrain but are well-suited for mountain operations. Successful units combine the basic doctrine described in FM 3-21.10 and augment with specialized equipment and predeployment training. The tactics and techniques specific to conducting operations in mountain terrain provide added operational capability. Table 6-3 in this manual depicts where Soldiers may obtain specialized mountaineering and cold weather operational skills.

This manual focuses on company and below operations in mountain operational terrain levels II and III as described in FM 3-97.6, specifically, where the influence of increasingly steep and rugged terrain dictates the use of dismounted operations. For mountain operations in level I (lower, less rugged valleys and flatter terrain) refer to FM 3-21.10. The concepts discussed in this publication are useful in most mountain environments.

This publication applies to the Active Army, the Army National Guard (ARNG)/Army National Guard of the United States (ARNGUS), and the United States Army Reserve (USAR) unless otherwise stated.

The proponent of this publication is the United States Army Training and Doctrine Command (TRADOC). The preparing agency is the US Army Maneuver Center of Excellence (MCoE). You may send comments and recommendations by any means—US mail, e-mail, fax, or telephone—using or following the format of DA Form 2028, *Recommended Changes to Publications and Blank Forms*. Point of contact information follows:

E-mail: BENN.CATD.DOCTRINE@CONUS.ARMY.MIL
Phone: COM 706-545-7114 or DSN 835-7114
Fax: COM 706-545-8511 or DSN 835-8511
US Mail: Commanding General, MCoE
           Directorate of Training and Doctrine (DOTD)
           ATTN: ATZB-TDD
           Fort Benning, GA 31905-5410

Unless stated otherwise, masculine nouns and pronouns refer to both male and female genders.

Chapter 1

Introduction

Combat in mountainous areas presents units with complicated and ever-shifting hazards, difficulties, opportunities, and risks. Mountain combat calls for extreme physical fitness, mental toughness, endurance, and the utmost in tactical and technical proficiency on the part of all individuals. A disciplined and prepared Infantry rifle company that is task-organized with and supported by the other members of the combined arms team is the key to successful small-unit mountain operations. A unit fighting in the mountains must overcome difficulties, measure risks, and exploit opportunities to close with the enemy and defeat him and well-prepared commanders anticipate, understand, and adapt to the physical demands of mountain environments. They face and overcome the challenges of fighting in areas where technological supremacy can be negated by even the most crude and non-technical enemy actions. Commanders who know what to expect during mountain operations create situations that allow their companies to adapt to the challenges and achieve victory on all battlefields.

REFERENCES

1-1.   Table 1-1 consolidates the references to additional information.

Table 1-1. Guide for subjects referenced in text

Subject	References
Mountain Operations	FM 3-97.6
Military Mountaineering	FM 3-97.61

OVERVIEW

1-2.   Infantry companies conducting offensive, defensive, and stability operations in mountain terrain are able to adapt and skillfully use the environmental challenges to their advantage. The design of the landscape, coupled with climatic conditions, creates a unique set of mountain operations characteristics that are characterized by—

- Close fights with dismounted Infantry. Mountain combat is often close in nature as the opposing forces meet in the rugged terrain. Even though engaging targets near the limits of direct fire weapons does occur in mountain engagements, intervening crests, hills, ridges, gullies, depressions, and other terrain features often limit long range battles with the enemy. The upper levels of mountain terrain are characterized by a lack of trafficable roads. Use of motorized vehicles is often restricted, forcing mission execution to dismounted units.
- Decentralized small-unit operations. Conflicts in mountain environments are often fought on a platoon and squad level as the terrain commonly does not support the meeting and maneuver of large units. The compartmentalization of mountain terrain can separate brigades from battalions, battalions from companies, and companies from platoons for long periods. As altitude increases in mountain environments, the terrain generally becomes more rugged and restrictive which drives the need for decentralized execution of missions by dismounted platoons and squads.

- Degraded mobility and increased movement times. The ruggedness of mountain terrain often restricts mobility to foot movements using file type formations on roads and trails. A relatively short distance from point to point may be an arduous movement over steep, rocky, uneven terrain, with multiple trail switchbacks that increase the distance traveled and the energy expended to traverse it.
- Unique sustainment solutions. Sustainment in a mountain environment is a challenging and time-consuming process. Terrain and weather complicate virtually all sustainment operations including logistics resupply, medical and casualty evacuation, and Soldier health and hygiene. The network of restrictive mountain roads often does not support resupply vehicles with a large turning radius, or permit two-way traffic. Movement of supplies often involves a combination of movement types including air, vehicle, foot, and animal, with each technique having its own challenges in mountain environments.
- Operations in thinly populated areas. The populace lives in typical mountain environments live mostly in small villages in the valleys with some scattered villages in the upper mountain areas. Although the farmers and animal herders that make up a large majority of the indigenous population may work up in the mountains, the vast amount of mountain terrain remains unpopulated.

1-3. Mountain terrain and weather conditions can be both an advantage and a disadvantage to friendly or enemy forces. If unprepared, the terrain can also be a company's adversary. Personnel must prepare mentally and physically, and leaders must prepare tactically and logistically in order to effectively conduct missions in the mountains. Company leaders must understand physical characteristics of mountain environments, and how to use terrain and weather to their advantage.

1-4. Mountain terrain is characterized by one or more of the following:
- High altitudes.
- Gently rolling slopes to steep cliffs.
- Varying amounts of vegetation (heavy, light, or none).
- Timberline above which trees and bushes do not grow.
- Rocky ground.
- Wet or dry stream beds.
- Glaciated peaks.
- Compartmentalization.

1-5. Mountain weather is characterized by the following:
- Extreme conditions (such as scorching hot, sub freezing, violent thunderstorms, and blizzards).
- Large temperature differences between day and night.
- Sudden atmospheric disturbances.

INFANTRY COMPANY CAPABILITIES AND LIMITATIONS

1-6. Dismounted Infantry units conduct mountain operations best. The upper levels of mountain terrain severely limit or restrict vehicular movement and normally require dismounted operations. Mounted units assigned missions in mountain environments similarly have to dismount to complete the mission, using their vehicles for mission support when possible. Often only minor modifications to an Infantry rifle company's organic equipment are required for specific mountain environments or missions. These usually take the form of special clothing and equipment needed for cold weather and steep terrain.

1-7. Table 1-2 shows an Infantry rifle company's capabilities and limitations in mountain environments.

Table 1-2. Infantry rifle company capabilities and limitations in the mountains

Capabilities	Limitations
Conduct offensive and defensive operations.	Vulnerable to enemy artillery and air assets.
Seize, secure, occupy, and retain terrain.	Vulnerable to enemy chemical, biological, radiological, nuclear (CBRN) attacks with limited decontamination capability.
Destroy, neutralize, suppress, interdict, disrupt, block, canalize, and fix enemy forces.	
Breach enemy obstacles.	Slow movement in rocky, steep, uneven terrain.
Feint and demonstrate to deceive the enemy.	Vulnerable to fatigue easily in high altitudes.
Provide security for friendly units.	Increased sustainment challenges.
Reconnoiter, deny, bypass, clear, contain, and isolate. (These tasks might be oriented on both terrain and enemy.)	Vulnerable to sudden changes in weather and temperature.
Conduct decentralized platoon and squad operations.	
Participate in air assault operations.	
Operate in conjunction with special operations forces.	
Move across difficult terrain.	

MOUNTAIN OPERATIONS FUNDAMENTALS

1-8.   The company commander's mission analysis helps him decide how to conduct effective combat operations in a particular area of operations (AO). His analysis should ensure the company is operating in a way that capitalizes on the unique characteristics of mountain environments by using those characteristics to his advantage. The following fundamentals provide guidance for planning mountain operations.

CONDUCT SMALL-UNIT DECENTRALIZED OPERATIONS

1-9.   The mountain environment usually dictates that commanders conduct small-unit, decentralized operations. Mountain operations are normally characterized by noncontiguous AOs with centralized planning and decentralized command and control. Mountain terrain can span vast regions – often with great distances between populated areas. Long distances often separate companies operating in this terrain. In addition, compartmentalization of valleys and corridors due to high ridges and mountain peaks naturally divides the terrain and complicates movement between compartments. Rugged, steep, terrain that restricts mobility to foot movements does not offer many opportunities for movement and maneuver of large units. Even small-units are forced into file type formations during movement. While companies may operate as part of a larger force, combat engagements in higher level mountain terrain tend to be conducted by small-units.

USE TERRAIN AND WEATHER EFFECTIVELY

1-10. Typical terrain and weather conditions found in mountain environments demand modifications to tactical operations conducted on flatter, less rugged and less demanding terrain. In addition to widespread operations across great distances and multiple corridors, mountain operations include a vertical, as much or more, than a horizontal dimension. Friendly elements often engage the enemy on a different elevation than their own. Mountain ridges and terrain features that overlook the terrain below can be used to influence operations at those lower levels from both a friendly and enemy perspective. Higher ground often becomes key terrain and must be controlled by friendly forces to enhance offensive, defensive, and security operations.

1-11. Drastically changing weather conditions equally influence operations. Understanding current and potential weather conditions helps commanders visualize how weather may be used during mission planning for combat operations. Sudden or unexpected snowstorms, fog, rain, and other climatic conditions may impede planned operations but may also be used to aid in masking movements or creation of natural obstacles.

USE ALL AVAILABLE RECONNAISSANCE ASSETS

1-12. Reduced mobility, compartmented terrain, limited visibility in critical areas, and rapidly changing weather increases the importance of reconnaissance and security in the mountains. Since the enemy can easily be concealed in a mountain environment, all available reconnaissance assets should be employed to gain as much information as possible. Maps are frequently inaccurate or lacking in detail, making reconnaissance of an AO essential to developing an accurate description. Along with conventional reconnaissance units, excellent sources of information include aircraft crews, unmanned aircraft systems (UAS), and other units and personnel moving through or operating in a particular area. Large amounts of dead space require reconnaissance by some means to aid in operations.

MAINTAIN SECURITY

1-13. Companies must constantly provide for all-around security. During movement, the overwatching force, positioned on terrain that adequately covers the movement, covers the moving force. These forces may bound with the moving force or may be inserted by other means such as helicopters. When in a defensive position, ground patrols, observation posts, remote sensors, and other aerial and ground surveillance assets help provide security both during the day and during limited visibility. Mountain terrain provides great opportunities for enemy ambushes. Detailed planning of routes, control of terrain suited for an ambush, and preparation for actions on contact must accompany every movement. Companies must also consider the potential threats imposed from the natural air avenues of approach that traverse their AO. If an active enemy air threat is present, higher commands control these areas in order to maintain security from enemy air assets and to facilitate friendly air operations.

INTEGRATE AVAILABLE AIR ASSETS

1-14. Fixed-wing and rotary-wing aircraft are vital combat assets in mountain operations. Planning for the use of supporting fires from air assets in conjunction with artillery and mortar indirect fires is critical for mountain offensive and defensive operations. Air assets can attack targets in areas difficult or impossible to reach by ground indirect fire. Air assets are also used extensively for tactical reconnaissance and movement of troops and supplies. Rotary-wing aircraft are commonly used in air assault operations to quickly insert and pick up personnel in difficult mountain terrain. Air delivery of supplies is often the only feasible means of resupply to companies operating at high altitudes in rough mountain terrain.

1-15. The use of utility and attack rotary-wing aircraft is prevalent in mountainous terrain. Various restrictions, such as weather, security and safety, cargo size, and number of personnel to be transported, can be limiting factors and make operations difficult. Coordination and quality communication with the aircrews prior to mission execution can lessen these restrictions. The further in advance that coordination can be made, the more likely aircrews are able to completely support the ground mission.

MOUNTAIN ENVIRONMENT

1-16. An operational environment is a composite of the conditions, circumstances, and influences that affect employment capabilities and bear on the decisions of the commander. Battalion and higher level staff develop that information specific to a particular environment during the intelligence preparation of the battlefield (IPB) process and provide the analysis to the company. The IPB consists of a four-step process that includes—

- Defining the operational environment.
- Describing environmental effects on operations.
- Evaluating the threat.
- Determining enemy courses of action.

1-17. While each environmental analysis is unique, especially as it applies to a particular enemy and mission, there are some environmental aspects that apply to most mountain environments. The following discussion focuses on those elements in the first two steps of the IPB process that pertain to the physical characteristics of mountains and their effects on mountain operations.

OPERATIONAL CHARACTERISTICS

1-18. There is no simple system to classify mountain environments. Soil composition, surface configuration, elevation, latitude, and climatic patterns determine the specific characteristics of each major mountain range. The operational environment of mountains includes information and people, as well as physical areas. Operational variables describe the operational environment. Commanders use them to understand and analyze the environment in which they are conducting operations. The variables describe not only the military aspects of the operational environment but also the population's influence on it. The variables are political, military, economic, social, information and infrastructure, with the addition of physical environment and time (PMESII-PT). While most of the variables can only be discussed as they pertain to a specific mountain environment, a discussion of the physical environment including the terrain, climate, and general discussion of the mountain population can be applied to all mountains.

Mountain Terrain

1-19. Commanders and leaders should first understand the characteristics of mountain terrain in order to determine their application to combat operations. For the purposes of U.S. Army military operations, mountains are classified as landforms that rise more than 500 meters above the surrounding plain and are characterized by steep slopes. Mountains may consist of an isolated peak, single ridges, glaciers, snowfields, compartments, or complex ranges extending for long distances and obstructing movement. (See FM 3-97.6 and FM 3-97.61 for more details.)

Operational Terrain Levels

1-20. Mountain operations are generally carried out at three operational terrain levels. (FM 3-97.6 describes operational terrain levels I, II, and III with more detail.) See Figure 1-1.

Level I

1-21. Level I terrain is located at the bottom of valleys and along the main lines of communications. At this level, mounted forces can operate, but maneuver space is often restricted. Dismounted and mounted forces are normally combined, since vital lines of communication usually follow the valley highways, roads, and trails. Most, but not all, of the civilian population is found at this level.

Level II

1-22. Level II terrain lies between valleys and shoulders of mountains. Generally, narrow roads and trails, which serve as secondary lines of communication, cross this ridge system. Ground mobility is difficult. Additionally, since dismounted forces can easily influence operations at level I from level II, they often expend great effort on these ridges. Similarly, enemy positions at the next level can threaten operations on these ridges. The enemy can often find sanctuary at this level in the form of bunkers and caves.

Level III

1-23. Level III includes the dominant terrain of summit regions. Although summit regions may contain relatively gentle terrain, mobility in level III is usually the most difficult to achieve and maintain. Level III terrain can provide opportunities for well-trained units to attack the enemy from the flanks and rear. At this terrain level, acclimatized Soldiers with proper skills and equipment can infiltrate to attack lines of communication, logistics bases, air defense sites, and command and control facilities.

Figure 1-1. Operational terrain levels I, II, & III

Terrain Characteristics

1-24. Mountains may rise abruptly from the plains to form a giant barrier or ascend gradually as a series of parallel ridges extending unbroken for great distances. They may consist of varying combinations of isolated peaks, rounded crests, eroded ridges, high plains, cut valleys, gorges, and deep ravines. Major mountain ranges are extremely complex. Regardless of the specific type, mountain terrain is considered rugged. Mountain terrain is characterized in terms of hydrological (water) data, elevation data, soil composition, and vegetation.

Hydrology

1-25. Mountains are home to a number of water sources including fresh water springs, lakes, and streams. Mountain stream beds may be dry or contain a significant amount of water. Smaller stream beds often feed into larger ones at roughly perpendicular angles, and are fed by mountain springs and runoff from melting snow or rain. Flash floods from storms in mountain stream beds are common.

1-26. In winter and at higher elevations throughout the year, snow may blanket slopes, creating an environment or condition of its own. Steep, snow-covered terrain presents the risk of snow avalanches as well. Arctic and subarctic mountain environments, as well as the upper elevations of the world's high mountains, may contain vast areas of glaciation. Valleys in these areas are frequently buried under massive glaciers and present hazards such as hidden crevices.

Elevation

1-27. Mountains have a natural lay of the land that separates distinct sections of terrain. They can be steep, making the terrain exceptionally difficult to traverse. Slopes commonly range from 4 to 45 degrees. Cliffs and precipices may be vertical or overhanging. Mountain ridges, valley floors, and intervening hills and crests naturally break the region up into smaller compartments, and channel movement through naturally created corridors. Mountain peaks can range to very high elevations with their surfaces generally composed of varying combinations of rock, snow, and ice.

Soil

1-28. Mountain ground is usually rocky consisting of various types of rock. These rocks can be loose and unstable and formed on varying degrees of slopes compounding movement across them. Many slopes are scattered with rocky debris deposited from the higher peaks and ridges. Extensive rock or boulder fields are known as talus. Slopes covered with smaller rocks, usually fist-sized or smaller, are called scree fields.

Vegetation

1-29. While trees and vegetation are commonly found at or near the base of mountains, on ascending slopes, and lower ridges and hilltops, there is a certain elevation past which they cannot thrive. This elevation – characterized by cold temperatures, insufficient air pressure, and lack of moisture – is known as the timberline. Depending on the latitude and region, the timberline generally occurs between 2300 and 4000 meters (7500 and 13,000 feet). In the Hindu Kush Mountains in Afghanistan, for example, the timberline occurs at approximately 3300 meters (10,800 feet).

1-30. Aside from obvious rock formations and other local vegetation characteristics, actual slope surfaces of mountains are usually found as some type of relatively firm earth or grass. Grassy slopes may include grassy clumps known as tussocks, short alpine grasses, or tundra. Tundra is most common at higher elevations and latitudes. The hills are often covered with trees and bushes below the timberline. In winter and spring, the sun dries out southern mountain slopes - leaving less water for plant life to flourish. Because the northern side of a hill tends to hold more water, vegetation is generally thicker. On gentle slopes, trees may also be thicker but as the slope increases, trees become more widely spread.

Mountain Climate

1-31. Equal to an understanding of terrain characteristics, leaders should know the characteristics of mountain climates before determining their military application. By understanding mountain climate characteristics, leaders can take advantage of the opportunities offered by current weather conditions while minimizing the adverse effects on operations and personnel.

1-32. Mountain climates are characterized in terms of visibility, wind velocity, precipitation, cloud cover, temperature, humidity, and atmospheric pressure. These mountain climates often span a wide range of conditions that may include strong winds, thin air, intense solar and ultraviolet radiation, deep snow, raging thunderstorms, blizzards, heavy fog, and rapidly changing weather. Weather conditions can change suddenly and unexpectedly in the mountains, and temperatures at high altitudes can range from very hot to extremely cold in the course of one day. Severe storms can cut off outside contact for a week or longer. Avalanches and rockslides are not uncommon. In addition, mountains can create their own microclimates or areas in which the climate differs from the prevailing climate in the surrounding area.

Visibility

1-33. Light data charts can provide times for sunrise, sunset, and morning and evening twilight hours for the local area. Other factors that affect visibility include weather conditions such as rain and snow storms, clouds, and fog. Fog in mountains is much the same as in other terrain but occurs more frequently and can remain for long periods. Mountain winds often result in blowing snow, sand, or debris that further impairs visibility. On clear days, high elevations provide opportunities to see for great distances.

Wind velocity

1-34. Valleys are usually protected from strong winds, while ridges and passes of mountains are seldom calm. Wind velocity generally increases with altitude and is intensified by mountain terrain. Valley breezes moving up a slope are more common in the morning, while descending mountain breezes are more common in the evening. Wind speed increases when winds are forced over ridges and peaks, or when funneled through narrowing mountain valleys, passes, and canyons. Exposed mountainsides and summits are especially subject to strong winds.

Precipitation

1-35. As mountain elevation increases, so does the amount of precipitation. Mountain ranges set natural conditions that cause a rapid rise of large amounts of air. As this air rises, the decrease in atmospheric pressure and temperature causes frequent rain and thunderstorms. As it continues to pass over mountains, it creates distinct local weather patterns. Precipitation also occurs more often on the windward side of mountain ranges than on the leeward side. A heavily wooded belt usually marks the zone of maximum precipitation. Snow is common in the mountains and depending on the specific region, may occur at anytime during the year at elevations above 1500 meters (5000 feet). Heavy rains and rapidly thawing snow and ice can create flash floods many miles downstream from the actual location of the rain or snow.

1-36. Inclement weather can appear quickly and change the nature of planned operations with little notice. Indicators of approaching inclement weather (within twenty-four to forty-eight hours) include—

- A gradual lowering of clouds.
- An increasing halo around the sun or moon.
- An increase in humidity or temperature.
- A decrease in barometric pressure.
- Strong winds (blowing snow off peaks).

1-37. Local thunderstorms usually last only a short time. Interior ranges with continental climates are more conducive to thunderstorms than coastal ranges with maritime climates. In alpine zones, driving snow and sudden wind squalls often accompany thunderstorms. Ridges and peaks become focal points for lightning strikes, and the occurrence of lightning is greater in the summer than the winter.

1-38. Storms resulting from widespread atmospheric disturbances often involve strong winds and heavy precipitation, and are the most severe weather conditions to occur in the mountains. These conditions may last several days, even longer than in the lowlands. Specific conditions vary depending on the path of the storm. Colder weather impedes clearing of these storms at high elevations. Winter storms in alpine regions are usually accompanied by low temperatures, high winds, and blinding snow.

Cloud cover

1-39. Clouds are common in mountain environments and may form quickly. Unlike lower elevations, clouds may come in contact with a portion of the mountain. Clouds are formed when warm air blowing against the side of a mountain is forced upward and cools. These clouds often lead to rain or snow storms.

Temperature

1-40. Air temperature decreases as elevation increases in the mountains. Wind and other climatic conditions also have an effect on mountain environment temperatures. Mountain microclimates create conditions where temperatures may range from scorching hot during the day to below freezing at night.

Humidity

1-41. Humidity in mountain environments is often lower than at sea level. At higher elevations, air is considerably drier because cold air cannot hold as much moisture as warm air.

Atmospheric pressure

1-42. Atmospheric pressure decreases with an increase in elevation. The decrease in atmospheric pressure spreads oxygen molecules further apart, resulting in a decrease of oxygen in each breath a person takes. A decrease in air pressure results in a decrease in air temperature and an increase in relative humidity.

Mountain Population

1-43. The populace in a mountain environment includes civilian as well as government and military personnel. A large majority of the indigenous population in mountain environments are rural people such as farmers and animal herders that live mostly in small villages in the valleys. Enemy personnel can easily blend into this population.

1-44. Host nations may have a variety of government and military personnel with which U.S. forces must operate. In Afghanistan for instance, the Afghan National Security Forces include the Afghan National Army, the Afghan National Police, and Afghan Security guards.

EFFECTS ON OPERATIONS

1-45. Mountain terrain and weather affect nearly every aspect of mountain operations. The effects of mountain terrain on mobility and movement are covered in detail in Chapter 5 of this manual. The physical characteristics of mountains—

- Affect mobility and lengthen movement times.
- Tax Soldiers both physically and mentally.
- Affect the operation and accuracy of some weapons.
- Challenge sustainment operations.
- Create hazards and risks.
- Complicate medical evacuation (MEDEVAC)/casualty evacuation (CASEVAC) operations.
- Interfere with line of sight communications.
- Challenge command and control.

1-46. In preparation for combat, commanders should consider the following list of specialized operations, procedures, and techniques that may be required for successful operations in mountain terrains:

- Basic climbing techniques.
- Mountain navigation.
- Mountain stream crossing.
- Long-range angle firing techniques.
- Mountain terrain route selection.
- Off-road and steep-terrain driving.
- Use of ropes (fixed ropes, high lines, and basic installations).
- Procedures to avoid landslides and avalanches.
- Use of animal transport for weapons and logistical items.
- Walking and movement techniques for steep and rough terrain.
- Cold weather movement (snowshoe movement and sled operations).
- Mountain survival techniques.
- Hazardous cross country night movement.
- Advanced first aid.
- Personal hygiene and field sanitation.
- Small unit standard operating procedure (SOP) and immediate action drills.
- Rough terrain/steep earth CASEVAC.
- Landing zone/pick up zone selection and control in restrictive terrain.

1-47. Commanders focus their operational analysis on specific elements of the environment that apply to their particular mission. Upon receipt of a mission, they narrow their focus to six mission variables. These variables include mission, enemy, terrain and weather, troops and support available, time available, and civil considerations (METT-TC) and are used to conduct mission analysis. Commanders conduct detailed terrain and weather analysis, as well as an analysis of the other factors of METT-TC, for each particular mission.

1-48. Mountain environments can affect all of the warfighting functions, including movement and maneuver, intelligence, fires, sustainment, command and control, and protection. These effects are discussed throughout the remaining chapters of this manual as they apply to one or more of the warfighting functions.

This page intentionally left blank.

Chapter 2

Command and Control

Commanders exercise command and control (C2) over assigned and attached forces during the accomplishment of a mission. C2 continues throughout the operations process of planning, preparation, execution, and assessment. Like any other environment, commanders in mountain environments exercise command by understanding, visualizing, describing, directing, leading, and assessing during the operations process. While the exercise of C2 itself does not change in the mountains, the application of C2 can be significantly affected by the physical environment.

REFERENCES

2-1.   Table 2-1 consolidates the references to additional information.

Table 2-1. Guide for subjects referenced in text

Subject	References
Operations	FM 3-0
The Infantry Rifle Company	FM 3-21.10
Basic Cold Weather Manual	FM 31-70
Intelligence Preparation of the Battlefield	FM 2-01.3
The Operations Process	FM 5-0
Risk Management Guide	USARAK Pamphlet 385-4
Composite Risk Management	FM 5-19
Operational Terms and Graphics	FM 1-02

LEADERSHIP

2-2.   Leadership is a critical component to successful mountain operations. No amount of technology or equipment can take the place of competent leadership. Competent leaders understand the unique characteristics of mountains and the demands of mountain environments. Leaders must recognize and address physical and mental fatigue in their Soldiers. In mountain environments, small mistakes can lead to catastrophic events. Leaders must ensure Soldiers maintain mental alertness and pay attention to detail during all operations. Loss of concentration during a difficult mountain climb, for example, may cause unit personnel to overlook suspicious signs of enemy personnel or activity, or could lead to a slip and fall down a steep mountain cliff resulting in serious injury.

2-3.   Distances between parent and subordinate units can be great in mountain environments and the demand for junior leaders to exercise leadership, decision-making, and initiative becomes increasingly paramount. In conflicts involving non-contiguous AOs, commanders at the company level often have expanded responsibility in a particular location far removed from a neighboring unit. This environment demands that junior leaders take charge, manage their personnel, and maintain mental toughness beyond what they experience in many other environments.

2-4.   During mountain operations, junior leaders often direct command post operations and conduct missions while separated by great distances from their parent unit for extended periods. They will be required to make tough choices between their Soldiers' physical capabilities and mission accomplishment. Leaders who have previously served in the mountains are a great source of information for junior leaders as they already have an understanding of what it takes to plan, prepare, and execute missions in this type of environment.

2-5. Junior leaders must also understand the capabilities, limitations, and employment of weapon systems, platforms, and resources often used by senior commanders in order to use them effectively. These include sniper teams, artillery, mortars, forward observers, close combat attack (CCA), close air support (CAS), UAS, and other attachments such as civil affairs, military information support operations teams, military police, engineers, explosive ordinance disposal teams, and interpreters.

LEADERSHIP IN ADVERSE WEATHER

2-6. A unique challenge for leaders in the mountain environment is the potential for operations in extreme weather and temperature conditions. The process of developing Soldiers into cold weather fighters requires positive leadership. Leaders must understand the environmental threat and include plans for countering that threat in their operational plans or tactical standing operating procedures. Initially, the environment may be alarming and even frightening to Soldiers unaccustomed to operating in typical mountain weather conditions, especially when deployed to unfamiliar, remote areas. Some Soldiers may find themselves confronted with challenges they have never encountered. The weather is a constant reminder to the Soldier of his vulnerability in the extreme environment and the likelihood of him becoming a casualty should he make a mistake. As Soldiers gain experience, they develop confidence in themselves, their clothing and equipment, and learn they can fight and win in the mountains to defeat both the environment and the enemy.

2-7. Aggressive, positive leadership is essential in helping Soldiers overcome the challenges of adverse weather. To defeat the enemy, Soldiers should first learn how to live and survive the elements so they can focus on the enemy. Leaders should maintain a positive attitude toward the mission, their Soldiers, and their equipment.

2-8. Intense weather affects the mind as well as the body. For example, in extremely cold temperatures, Soldiers can become frustrated and mentally exhausted while attempting to perform tasks and keep warm at the same time. Essential tasks often take longer to perform and require more effort than in temperate climates. This should be considered when planning operations and giving orders. Even routine tasks such as vehicle maintenance and making or striking camp require an increase in time. There is no simple formula for the extra time required to accomplish tasks. The time needed varies with differing conditions, the state of training, and the degree of acclimatization of the troops. It should not be used as an excuse for over-insurance. Troops readied unnecessarily early or left standing in the open after striking camp may suffer physically. Such overcompensation can also affect Soldier morale.

COMMAND

2-9. Command is the authority that a commander exercises over his unit. It includes the responsibility for effectively using available resources and planning, organizing, directing, coordinating, and controlling his unit to accomplish assigned missions.

2-10. Command and control are interrelated. The exercise of C2 by commanders conducting mountain operations is greatly affected by the terrain itself. Widely dispersed AOs and physically demanding topography challenges C2 as well as communications systems in a mountain environment. Leaders at all levels should mentally prepare themselves for these conditions.

2-11. Leaders should also be familiar with the composite risk management process used in decision-making. Composite risk management helps mitigate risks associated with all threats and hazards that have the potential to injure or kill personnel, destroy equipment, or otherwise affect mission effectiveness. (See FM 5-19 and USARAK Pamphlet 385-4 for details.)

BATTLE COMMAND

2-12. FM 3-0 describes commanders conducting battle command as understanding, visualizing, describing, directing, leading, and assessing during the course of operations. The company commander performs these actions continuously to directly influence operations in their AO. While the company command post (CP) is there to assist, the commander cannot conduct battle command from the CP itself. He should locate himself in a position where he can best influence operations.

COMPANY COMMAND POST

2-13. The company CP assists the commander in controlling operations and planning. The CP is austere in comparison to higher echelon CPs, and it has less capability to integrate enablers, plan future operations, or perform other functions associated with more robust CPs. The company CP can assist the commander by maintaining communications with higher headquarters, adjacent units, and subordinate elements. It can also develop and submit routine and recurring reports to the battalion. The company CP can assist the commander during planning by performing tasks such as analyzing portions of the battalion order or developing specific parts of the company plan. The CP is composed of vehicles equipped with communications equipment and Force XXI Battle Command, Brigade-and-Below. It is the control station for the company command net that monitors the battalion command, operations, and sustainment nets.

2-14. The company CP locates where it can best support the company commander while maintaining communication with higher and subordinate units. To maintain communications, the CP may need to locate away from the company itself. In this case, the executive officer (XO) controls the CP (or part of it) and maintains communications with higher or adjacent units while the commander locates where he can best control the company. Although the CP can move independently, it normally locates where it is secured by other platoons and sections within the company. In mountain environment conflicts, company CPs are most often located in a combat outpost.

2-15. The company CP normally consists of the company commander, his radio operators, the fire support team, the CRBN non-commissioned officer (NCO), and other select personnel and attachments such as the XO, first sergeant, or a security element. The fire support team includes the fire support officer, fire support NCO, and forward observer. Company CPs often integrate the use of the company intelligence support team (COIST). (For more details on combat outposts and COISTs, see Chapter 6 of this manual.)

CONTROL

2-16. Control allows commanders to adjust their operations to conform to their commander's intent as conditions change. Commanders use both procedural (orders, regulations, policies, and doctrine) and positive (actively assessing, deciding, and directing) control during mountain operations. The use of positive control becomes more restrictive in mountain environments when there is a large dispersion between units.

2-17. Successful operations depend on how well leaders control their units. Control is sometimes limited to a well thought-out plan and thorough preparation. Commanders should develop a clear vision of how the operation may unfold, anticipate the decisive points, and place themselves at critical locations which may include heights overlooking the company operations.

2-18. Movements of large units in mountain terrain are difficult to synchronize due to the restrictive topography, the ability to change the axis of advance, and the ability to have mutually supporting axial. If the company is moving as part of a larger force, senior leaders should allow for realistic time estimates for movement when executing missions based on timetables. Thorough reconnaissance and experience can help leaders determine the time needed.

2-19. Mountain operations usually require centralized planning and decentralized execution of missions to accomplish the higher commander's intent. Decision-making authority is often pushed to the lowest level possible in this type of decentralized and dispersed operation. Decentralized mission execution allows commanders to conduct missions that effectively meet the commander's intent with the flexibility of incorporating current conditions into his decisions and actions. During mission planning and execution, leaders should exercise control of all assigned and attached units in their area while fully understanding the higher level commander's intent.

COMMUNICATIONS

2-20. Terrain and unpredictable weather conditions affect communications at high altitudes. While unobstructed line-of-sight (LOS) radio communication conditions are excellent in the mountains, they are often difficult to achieve due to mountain ridges, intervening crests, and peaks. These terrain obstructions frequently interfere with LOS, very high frequency (VHF) radio communications such as the single channel ground and airborne radio system. Units can be in the bottom of a depression 1 km away from another unit and not be able to communicate. At other times, they may be on a mountaintop and able to communicate throughout the AO. Mountain terrain not only interferes with ground-to-ground communications but also can interfere with air-to-ground and air-to-air communications as well.

2-21. In addition to LOS issues, extreme operating distances further complicate frequency modulation (FM) communications in mountain environments. Terrain and distance combined often complicate FM communications to the point that they become ineffective or unreliable.

2-22. Commanders should understand the limitations that mountains and mountain climates place on communications systems. They should adapt to these conditions and find avenues around these limitations which allow units to effectively communicate. Various possibilities for establishing communications should be considered to aid in communication efforts. Some communications techniques and systems that have been used in mountain environments to assist in LOS and other communications issues include—

- Moving to regain LOS with the receiver.
- Relaying transmissions from station to station.
- Employing retransmissions (RETRANS) stations.
- Using commercial radios.
- Using cell phones.
- Using couriers.

2-23. Communications planning in mountain terrain should include—

- Identifying problems ahead of time through a map reconnaissance and information gained through intelligence.
- Coordinating with adjacent units and aircraft.
- Using RETRANS stations.
- Obtaining additional batteries due to the increase in battery usage.
- Employing P.A.C.E. Plan (Primary, Alternate, Contingency, and Emergency backup systems and ensure dissemination).

COMMUNICATIONS EQUIPMENT

2-24. When using VHF radios in the mountains, units may consider using single-channel plain text to increase range. Automatic frequency hopping and encryption can be used but may decrease range. Battery power can decline quickly in extreme cold temperatures. Lithium batteries typically have more power and last longer than standard alkaline batteries and should be considered for routine issue. (For additional cold weather impacts on communications, see FM 31-70.)

2-25. RETRANS stations can be used to assist in VHF communications. These stations allow using units with LOS to the RETRANS site, but not to each other, the ability to communicate with VHF radios. Common LOS radios include the—

- AN/PRC-119 SINCGARS.
- AN/PRC-119 ASIPS.
- AN/PRC-148 MBITR.

2-26. In mountain environments, satellite communications and the use of C2 aircraft or unmanned RETRANS aircraft can offset some terrain limitations and reduce reliance on bulky less effective radio equipment. To assist in communications efforts, beyond line of sight radios are often employed. Units may also consider high frequency communications systems that are not LOS dependent. Harris radios such as the AN/PRC 150 that operate in the high frequency band as well as tactical satellite (TACSAT) radios that operate in the ultrahigh frequency band have frequently been used in mountain operations. These radios have the ability to communicate over vast distances and do not require LOS between using units. The TACSAT system is relatively easy to operate, but it requires operators speak in deliberate conversation. Commanders should be aware that the availability of channels may limit the use of TACSAT communications. TACSAT communications can be conducted using the—

- AN/PRC 117F.
- AN/PSC-5C/D.
- MBITR as a SATCOM.
- SAT Phone.

RETRANSMISSION STATIONS

2-27. Retransmission stations can greatly assist in gaining better coverage for radio communications systems. These stations are often situated on the highest available peaks in order to provide optimal range and coverage (Figure 2-1). The use of VHF radio communications often requires the augmentation of carefully selected retransmission sites. These sites are located on (or cause the area to inevitably become) key terrain. Mountain peaks often become part of the communications infrastructure and are crowded with military, national, commercial radio, television, and telephone communications systems, sites, and relay towers. These areas also often tend to be best for establishing retransmission stations.

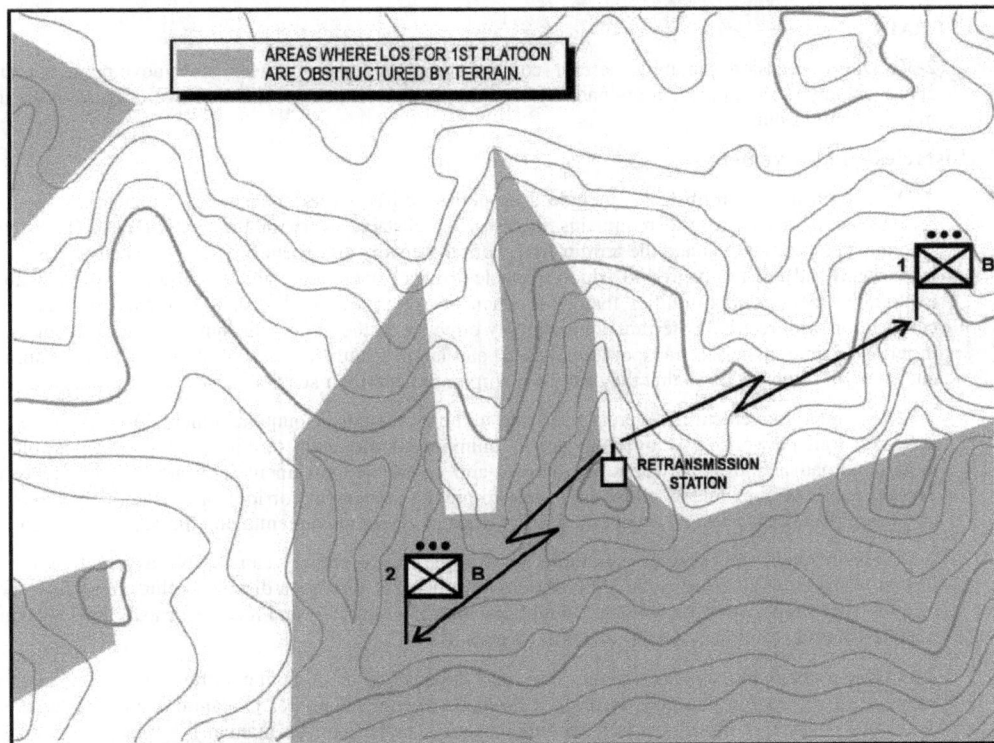

Figure 2-1. Retransmission station

2-28. Due to the terrain and weather conditions at these altitudes, crews responsible for installing and maintaining retransmission stations should be well trained in mountain survival techniques. Retransmission teams may also require specialized mountain mobility training and equipment to reach higher terrain. Isolated retransmission stations are prone to being targeted by the enemy and protection of these areas is a difficult but required operation. During employment of retransmission stations, commanders should consider—

- Availability of personnel required to operate the station.
- Availability of additional equipment.
- Security and sustainment of the station.
- Additional missions to include doubling as observation post (OP).

MISSION PLANNING

2-29. During mountain operations, commanders maintain procedural control of subordinate units largely through mission orders. Company commanders receive warning orders, operations orders, and fragmentary orders from the battalion and subsequently use troop-leading procedures (TLP) to generate his own orders to units within his command. The procedural steps for company level TLP covered in FM 3-21.10 and FM 5-0 are the same for mountain operations as with any other environment. Unique to mountain operations are those factors within TLP that pertain specifically to the terrain and weather analysis.

TERRAIN

2-30. During mission planning, terrain considerations include obstacles and movement, avenues of approach, key terrain, observation, and fields of fire, and cover and concealment with regard to the unique mountain environment.

Obstacles and Movement

2-31. Natural mountain obstacles include deep defiles, cliffs, rivers, landslides, avalanches, crevices, and scree slopes, as well as the mountains themselves. Obstacles vary in their effect on different forces. Commanders should evaluate the terrain from both the enemy and friendly force perspective. They should look specifically at the degree to which obstacles restrict operations, and at the ability of each force to exploit the tactical opportunities that exist when obstacles are employed. Man-made obstacles used in conjunction with restrictive terrain are extremely effective in the mountains, but their construction is costly in terms of time, materiel, transportation assets, and labor. Commanders should know the location, extent, and strength of obstacles so that they can be incorporated into their scheme of maneuver.

2-32. Mounted movement is severely restricted in the mountains. Mountain vehicle traffic is limited to the road and trail networks as movement across unimproved mountain terrain is next to impossible. Most mountain road and trail networks are narrow and constitute movement in nearly single file convoys. Terrain-restricted movements allow the enemy to predict movement corridors and effectively choose areas of engagement. Leaders must accept these risks when planning movement along limited-mobility corridors.

2-33. Harsh roads and weather conditions as well as enemy activity can disable a vehicle, creating an instant obstacle on a narrow path. Units should have plans to remove a disabled vehicle and clear the road or trail. Tow straps, tow bars, winches, sand bags, spill kits, shovels, and recovery capabilities for damaged vehicles should accompany all moving units if possible.

2-34. Dismounted movements can be slow and exhausting in mountain terrain. Traveling over steep, uneven, rugged terrain can quickly drain a Soldier's strength if proper precautions are not taken. (For a detailed discussion of movement in the mountains, see Chapter 5 of this manual.)

2-35. The compartmentalization of mountain terrain dictates the nature of mountain combat. Compartments are not necessarily large and units operating in these areas may become easily separated for extended periods. Compartmentalization effects on operations may include—

- Degraded ability to quickly switch to an alternate axis of advance.
- Difficulty in maintaining mutual support between units.
- Difficulty in moving reserve assets across the terrain.

- Increased difficulty in coordinating the battle in multiple mobility corridors.
- Difficulty in maintaining line of sight communications.
- Increased demands on junior leaders due to separation from higher level units.

Avenues of Approach

2-36. In mountain terrain, there are few easily accessible avenues of approach. Those that exist usually run along valleys, defiles, or on crests and spurs of ridges. This type of geography allows a defender to economize in difficult terrain and concentrate mainly on dangerous avenues of approach. A typical offensive tactic is to conduct a coordinated assault with the decisive operation along accessible avenues of approach, and shaping operations by one or more maneuver elements on difficult and unexpected avenues of approach. Normally, high rates of advance and heavy concentration of forces are difficult or impossible to achieve along mountain avenues of approach. Relief features may create large areas of dead space that facilitate covert movement. Units may seek to use difficult and unlikely avenues of approach to achieve surprise. These can be extremely high-risk operations and are prone to failure unless forces are well trained and experienced in mountaineering techniques. In mountain terrain, the analysis of avenues of approach should be based on a thorough reconnaissance and evaluated in terms of the following factors:

- Ability to achieve surprise.
- Vulnerability to attack from surrounding heights.
- Ability to provide mutual support to forces on other avenues of approach.
- Effect on rates of advance.
- Effect on command and control.
- Potential to accommodate deception operations.
- Ability to support necessary sustainment operations.
- Access to secure rest and halt sites.
- Potential to fix the enemy and reduce the possibility of retreat.

Key Terrain

2-37. Key terrain, as described by FM 1-02 as "any locality, or area, the seizure or retention of which affords a marked advantage to either combatant," may be found at any of the three operational terrain levels. Commanders and planners should clearly understand the effect operational terrain levels I, II, and III, as described in Chapter 1, have on operations and how each level influences the other. They should identify and control dominant terrain at each operational terrain level to facilitate maneuver of their units. Leaders should learn to visualize, describe, and direct operations vertically as well as horizontally. Key terrain generally increases in importance with an increase in elevation and a decrease in accessibility.

2-38. In the mountains, terrain that is higher than that held by the opposing force is often key, but only if the force is capable of fighting there. A well-prepared force capable of maneuver in rugged terrain can gain an even greater advantage over an ill-prepared enemy at higher elevation levels. The majority of operations in the mountains require that the commander designate decisive terrain in his concept of operations and to communicate its' importance to his staff and subordinate commanders. In operations over mountain terrain, the analysis of key and decisive terrain is based on the identification of these features at each of the three operational terrain levels. There are few truly impassable areas in the mountains. The commander should also recognize that what may be key terrain to one force may be an obstacle to another. He should also recognize that properly trained combatants can use high obstructing terrain as a means to achieve decisive victories with comparatively small-sized combat elements.

2-39. Controlling areas of lower elevations often means occupying those areas of key terrain above it such as mountain ridges. Keeping this in mind, crew-served weapons are often placed on high ridges and peaks where vehicle access is extremely limited. Surveillance assets such as the Improved Target Acquisition System (ITAS) and Long Range Advanced Scout Surveillance System (LRAS3), placed with crew-served weapons on high terrain can help control key passes and ridgelines. Pack animals may be used to carry these weapons to higher elevations. (See Chapter 6 for more on the use of pack animals.)

Observation and Fields of Fire

2-40. Although mountain terrain generally permits excellent long range observation and fields of fire, steep slopes and rugged terrain affect a Soldier's ability to accurately estimate range and frequently cause large areas to be hidden from observation. The existence of sharp relief and dead space facilitates covert approaches, making surveillance difficult despite such long-range observation. Factors that influence an individual's ability to observe and engage targets in mountain terrain are—

- Naturally-occurring dead space from hills, gullies, ravines, and other areas.
- Naturally-occurring weather conditions such as rain, fog, snow.
- The ability to observe and identify targets in conditions of bright sunlight.
- The ability to estimate range in clear air.
- The ability to apply wind corrections.
- The ability to shoot accurately up and down vertical slopes.

Cover and Concealment

2-41. The combination of trees, jagged rocks, and the folds of the earth offer excellent cover and concealment for friendly and enemy units alike. Small stream beds offer routes for ingress and egress as well as provide an environment for enemy activities including observation, communications relay, logistics, indirect fire, attacks, or ambushes.

2-42. The identification and proper use of the cover and concealment provided by mountain terrain is fundamental to all aspects of mountain operations. Ridge systems may provide covert approaches through many areas that are hidden from observation by the vegetation and relief. The difficulties a force encounters in finding available cover and concealment along ridges are fewer than those on the peaks, especially above the timberline. Uncovered portions of an approach leave a force exposed to observation and fire for long periods. The enemy can easily detect movement in these areas, leaving commanders with three primary options to improve cover and concealment as follows:

- Identify and exploit avenues of approach the enemy would consider unlikely, due to their difficult ascent or descent.
- Negotiate routes during limited visibility.
- Provide overwhelming route security.

WEATHER

2-43. Weather and visibility conditions in mountain environments may create unprecedented advantages and disadvantages for combatants. To fight effectively, commanders should acquire accurate weather information about their AO and be aware of changing weather conditions and common indicators of upcoming inclement weather.

2-44. Terrain has a dominant effect on local climate and weather patterns in the mountains. Mountain environments are subject to frequent and rapid changes of weather, including fog, strong winds, extreme heat or cold, and heavy rain or snow. Local mountains can create their own microclimates and therefore many forecasts that describe weather over large areas of terrain are inherently inaccurate for the mountains themselves. Commanders should be able to develop local, terrain based forecasts by combining available forecasts with field observations (local temperature, wind, precipitation, cloud patterns, barometric pressure, and surrounding terrain). Forecasting mountain weather from the field improves accuracy and enhances the ability to exploit opportunities offered by the weather, while minimizing its adverse effects.

2-45. During inevitable bad climate conditions in mountain environments, common task or operations become increasingly difficult to accomplish. If bad weather is expected or experienced, units should consider weather-related operational issues such as the early resupply of needed items or the adjustment of operations to accommodate the potential lack of resupply aircraft. Added effects for mountain environments as well as other inherent climate issues are shown in Table 2-2 below.

Table 2-2. Weather condition effects

Weather Condition	Flat to Moderate Terrain Effects	Added Mountain Effects
Sunshine	• Sunburn. • Snow blindness. • Temperature differences between sun and shade.	• Increased risk of sunburn and snow blindness. • Severe, unexpected temperature variations between sun and shade. • Avalanches.
Wind	• Wind chill.	• Increased risk and severity of wind chill. • Blowing debris or driven snow causing reduced visibility. • Avalanches.
Rain	• Reduced visibility. • Cooler temperatures.	• Landslides. • Flash floods. • Avalanches.
Snow	• Cold weather injuries. • Reduced mobility and visibility. • Snow blindness. • Blowing snow.	• Increased risk and severity of common effects. • Avalanches.
Storms	• Rain/snow. • Reduced visibility. • Lightning.	• Extended duration and intensity greatly affecting visibility and mobility. • Extremely high winds. • Avalanches.
Fog	• Reduced mobility/visibility.	• Increased frequency and duration.
Cloudiness	• Reduced visibility.	• Greatly decreased visibility at higher elevations.

2-46. Leaders and Soldiers should understand the need to be prepared for extreme climate changes while operating in the mountains. Environmental changes such as extreme cold, blizzards, fog, heavy rain downpours, flash floods, and lightning slow the pace of operations but can completely shut them down. Personnel should be ready for extreme cold, hot, windy, wet, and stormy conditions. Units may experience heat and cold injuries in the same day. They should be prepared for characteristic problems such as frostbite and snow blindness. (For additional information on cold weather operations, see FM 31-70.)

2-47. Personnel safety concerns are extremely heightened in mountain climates. Extra precautions should be taken to prevent heat, cold, and accidental injuries. During movements, extreme weather conditions can cause personnel to lose sight of roads, trails, markers, and other personnel. Snow can mask dangerous holes, cracks, and crevices. Roads and trails traditionally open for vehicle or foot traffic during summer months may be tactically closed during the winter. Spring rains can cause mountain creeks to swell and become extremely dangerous.

2-48. Weather conditions can have a drastic effect on all types of movement including dismounted, mounted, and air movements. Chapter 5 of this manual discusses the effects of mountain environments on movements in detail.

IPB PRODUCTS

2-49. To assist in mission planning, the company commander receives intelligence preparation of the battlefield products from the battalion that may include information on the following: (For detailed information, see FM 2-01.3.)

- Operational Environment.
    - Overlays (terrain, operational, demographic, infrastructure, economic, political).
    - Written products (threat study, demographic and cultural study, infrastructure reconnaissance, scientific and technical information, third nation support, banking, attitudes towards friendly and enemy forces, area history, and geography).
    - Charts and Graphics (areas, structures, capabilities, organizations, people, events).
- Environmental effects on operations.
    - Combined obstacle overlay.
    - Modified combined obstacle overlay.
    - Terrain and weather support.
- Threat Evaluation.
    - Organizations, equipment, and doctrine.
    - Threat tactics.
    - Capabilities.
    - Likely courses of action.

Chapter 3

Offensive Operations

In mountain environments, commanders seek to exploit an enemy's weakness by using the unique mountain characteristics to an offensive advantage. Offensive operations in mountains are conducted for three primary purposes: to deny an enemy a base of operations (sustainment, re-fit and C2) to conduct operations against U.S. or coalition forces; to isolate and defeat enemy forces before they are capable of operations in populated areas; and to secure lines of communication for friendly and coalition forces. During planning, commanders understand that even a technologically inferior enemy can capitalize on the advantages of mountain terrain and potentially mitigate U.S. forces' advantages in target acquisition, surveillance, firepower, and maneuver. This chapter discusses the tactics and techniques used for offensive operations in mountain environments and how the physical characteristics of mountains can support and enhance offensive missions.

REFERENCES

3-1. Table 3-1 consolidates the references to additional information.

Table 3-1. Guide for subjects referenced in text

Subject	References
Tactics	FM 3-90
The Infantry Rifle Company	FM 3-21.10
The Infantry Battalion	FM 3-21.20

OVERVIEW

3-2. A key factor in conducting offensive operations in mountain environments is first determining where the enemy is located or suspected to be. It is extremely difficult to target the enemy in rugged mountain terrain with physical characteristics such as caves, rock formations, depressions, rifts, and wooded areas. These offer excellent cover and concealment to light Infantry or paramilitary forces with a small vehicle, sustainment, and C2 footprint. The second major factor is determining an appropriate method to fix or place them in a kill zone where they can be attacked without their escaping.

3-3. As altitude increases in mountain environments, the terrain generally becomes more rugged and restrictive. This restriction drives most offensive combat operations to dismounted movements with smaller elements. Correspondingly, operations tend to become more decentralized and often take place at the platoon and squad level. Junior leadership initiative and decisiveness is essential during the conduct of these operations.

3-4. Leaders plan offensive engagements on favorable terms to the attacking force. As with all offensive operations, the initiative is with the attacker. The attacker chooses the time, place and method of attack, while the defender must consider all possible methods of attack and avenues of attack. With careful planning and preparation, units can execute effective attacks in the mountains. Understanding the enemy and how they use mountain terrain and weather to their advantage is crucial to developing a scheme of maneuver, and for creating clear tactical tasks with considerations for C2, time and additional combat power to support the mission. Leaders who understand enemy mountain tactics are better able to use the same mountain characteristics to their advantage.

CHARACTERISTICS

3-5.   The characteristics of the offense are surprise, tempo, concentration, and audacity. Commanders and leaders should understand how the mountain environment affects these characteristics in order to effectively plan and execute offensive missions in a mountain environment. Commanders who understand the impact mountain terrain has on planned operations, as well as the impact on potential actions the enemy may take when attacked, may use that knowledge to capitalize on developing the situation through anticipated contact and battle drills.

Surprise

3-6.   In the mountains, surprise is a major factor in achieving mission success in offensive operations. It is also more difficult to achieve than in many other environments. Units achieve surprise by striking the enemy at a time, place, or manner in which he is unprepared. While planning company, platoon, or squad movements, leaders should assume they will be observed by the enemy and plan for the necessary actions including use of terrain; dispersion; movement along more than one route or at different times; and movement during limited visibility conditions. In their planning, commanders and leaders must account for slow and tedious movements in restricted mountain terrain. Movements through restrictive mountain terrain during limited visibility can aid in the ability to achieve surprise. In addition, movement through an appropriate level of vertical terrain (for example, the use of a tree line or a ravine) may also achieve surprise. Weather conditions can also provide advantages during precipitation or fog. These conditions can cover movement, limit enemy observation, and help to achieve surprise.

3-7.   Surprise is also easier to obtain for the force that knows the terrain and has the skills and equipment necessary to achieve greater mobility. Mountain operations are fought on foreign soil against an enemy normally familiar with the area. Leaders closely analyze the terrain to determine how it may be used from an enemy perspective. Leaders then determine how the terrain can best be used in conjunction with movement (mounted, aerial, and ground) and maneuver reconnaissance and surveillance units and assets, engineer support, and fires) considerations for an offensive advantage to help achieve surprise. With a proper analysis of the terrain, leaders can also determine likely or possible points of contact, and develop and rehearse actions on contact to counter enemy actions.

Tempo

3-8.   Like surprise, tempo becomes increasingly difficult to maintain in the mountains as the terrain becomes more rugged and more restrictive. Tempo is the rate of military action relative to the enemy. Tempo is interrelated with surprise. Following an effective movement and attack, the commander can better control tempo and has more options for continued actions. Maintaining momentum and tempo retains the initiative, keeps the enemy off balance, contributes to the security of the attacking force, and prevents the defender from taking effective countermeasures.

3-9.   As in other environments, company commanders increase tempo by using simple plans, quick decision-making, decentralized control, mission orders, and rehearsed actions. The enemy depends on the restrictiveness of the terrain to slow the tempo of friendly units while they delay and break contact to reposition in new areas within the mountain environment. In mountain environments, commanders use task organization and combined arms assets to help offset enemy actions and maintain tempo. Artillery and air assets can deliver effective fires to maintain pressure on the enemy, allowing ground units increased time and space to maneuver. The commander may also consider—

* Attacking along a narrow front while frequently rotating the attacking element.
* Attacking along a narrow front to fix the enemy and, terrain permitting, using another element to maneuver to attack the enemy flank or rear.
* Attaching the mortar section or squads to the platoon with the main effort.

Concentration

3-10. Concentration of combat power is essential in mountain operations. Commanders plan offensive missions that can quickly concentrate combat power on the enemy before he has a chance to escape or counterattack. Commanders use combined arms assets to target enemy positions, fixing and obscuring their forces. This enables the commander to maneuver his unit through gaps and to the flanks (rear) of the enemy to increase the effectiveness of their attack.

3-11. It is important to understand that mountain terrain and climate conditions that affect friendly forces similarly affect the enemy. When conditions are favorable and the assets are available, artillery and air assets brought to bear on an enemy defensive position or an enemy attempting to escape on foot through rugged mountain terrain can be devastating. Concentration of combined arms assets can help confuse the enemy, cause him to fight in more than one direction, and cause him to alter his planned actions, further exposing his vulnerabilities. Conversely weather can affect the availability of fixed- and rotary-wing aircraft as well as their ability to effectively observe and engage targets. Terrain and soil conditions can hinder delivery of artillery based on the angle of the projectile and type of round/fuze being used.

Audacity

3-12. Audacity is a simple plan of action, boldly executed. Boldness and calculated risks are key factors to successful offensive operations. In the mountains, commanders use initiative and innovative thinking to develop schemes of maneuver that capitalize on the other characteristics of surprise, tempo, and concentration. For example, the commander may choose an unexpected axis or route of attack, such as a difficult approach up a steep slope toward an enemy location, to achieve surprise.

3-13. An audacious commander plans offensive missions with calculated risks that allow his company to maintain the advantage, reduce friendly casualties, and accomplish the mission. His actions, although quick and decisive, are based on a reasoned approach to the tactical situation and on his knowledge of his Soldiers, the enemy, and the unique considerations of mountain terrain.

TYPES

3-14. Offensive missions in mountain environments normally consist of the four types as described in FM 3-90, including attack, movement to contact (MTC), exploitation, and pursuit. Companies can execute an attack or an MTC in the mountains. Infantry companies will likely only participate in a higher unit's exploitation or pursuit, but even these operations are difficult in rugged mountain terrain.

Attack

3-15. An attack is an offensive operation that destroys the enemy, seizes or secures terrain, or both. During mountain operations, an Infantry company most often participates in a synchronized hasty or deliberate attack as part of a battalion or larger operation where the defeat of a specific force or control of some terrain is the decisive operation. Generally, company level attacks are more often in the form of special-purpose attacks, either a raid or an ambush, where the retention of terrain is not an objective.

Movement to Contact

3-16. An MTC is a type of offensive operation designed to establish or regain contact with the enemy with the intent on initiating an attack if the force is within the capability of the friendly unit. A company conducts an MTC when the enemy situation is vague, or not specific enough to conduct an attack, and maneuver space supports the operation. In the mountains where maneuver space is limited, an MTC may be conducted by an even smaller element, such as a platoon, if an engagement with the enemy is expected to be within its' capabilities. Canalizing mountain terrain that limits maneuver may lead commanders toward conducting reconnaissance patrols as opposed to MTCs with the intent on gathering information and developing the situation for a company hasty attack.

Exploitation

3-17. Exploitations are conducted at the brigade or higher level. Exploitation is a type of offensive operation that usually follows a successful attack and is designed to disorganize the enemy. Exploitations seek to disintegrate the enemy to where they have no alternative but surrender or fight. Companies may participate in a higher unit's exploitation. (See FM 3-21.20, for more details on exploitations.)

Pursuit

3-18. Pursuits are normally conducted at the brigade or higher level. A pursuit is an offensive operation designed to catch or cut off a hostile force attempting to escape, with the aim of destroying it. A pursuit typically follows a successful exploitation. Ideally, it prevents a fleeing enemy from escaping and then destroys him. Companies and platoons participate in a larger unit's exploitation and may conduct attacks as part of the higher unit's operation. (See FM 3-21.20, for more details on pursuits.)

SEQUENCE

3-19. Offensive operations in mountain environments follow the same sequence as operations conducted in other environments (See FM 3-90, for more details.) The sequence of offensive operations may be conducted simultaneously or sequentially, depending on mission variables, and are not the only way to conduct offensive operations. Normally the first three of these steps are shaping operations, while the maneuver step is the decisive operation. The follow through step is normally a sequel or a branch to the plan based on the revised situation. The sequence for conducting offensive operations in the mountains is:

- Gain and maintain enemy contact.
- Disrupt the enemy.
- Fix the enemy.
- Maneuver.
- Follow through.

Gain and Maintain Enemy Contact

3-20. Gaining and maintaining contact with the enemy is vital to the success of offensive operations. The manner in which the company gains and maintains contact depends on whether they are in contact with the enemy's security area or the enemy's main line of resistance. This typically involves making a physical reconnaissance of the objective using internal and external assets as the tactical situation permits. If available, UAS can provide accurate real-time reconnaissance of the objective. It also involves making a map reconnaissance of the objective and all the terrain that affects the mission. Additionally, units should analyze aerial imagery, photographs, or any other detailed information about the mountain terrain for which the unit is responsible.

3-21. The commander uses all available sources of information to find the enemy's location and dispositions to ensure the company is committed under optimal conditions. The enemy situation becomes clearer as the security elements conduct actions on contact to rapidly develop the situation in accordance with the commander's plan and intent.

Movement to the Line of Departure.

3-22. When attacking from positions not in contact, companies often stage in assembly areas, road march to attack positions behind friendly units in contact with the enemy, conduct passage of lines, and begin the attack. When attacking from positions in direct contact, the company line of departure is the same as the line of contact. In certain circumstances (noncontiguous mountain operations), there may not be a line of departure.

Approach to the Objective

3-23. The commander plans the approach to the objective to ensure security, speed, and flexibility. They select routes, techniques, formations, and methods that best support actions on the objective. All leaders must recognize this portion of the battle as a fight, not a movement. The company may have to fight through enemy combat forces, obstacles, artillery strikes, security elements, possible spoiling attacks, and other combat multipliers to reach the objective. The commander employs techniques that avoid the enemy's strength when possible and conceal the company's true intentions. He tries to deceive the enemy as to the location of the decisive operation, uses surprise to take advantage of his initiative in determining the time and place of his attack, and uses indirect approaches when available to strike the enemy from a flank or the rear. Mountain terrain challenges effective movement. Steep slopes, rock formations, and constant vertical changes to the landscape make movement and maneuver a difficult task. Units are often restricted to roads and trails that confine movements to file formations. Maneuver against an enemy using these likely avenues of approach are most likely observed. Company commanders should consider covering all movement in the mountains with an overwatching element due to the inherent risks associated with enemy use of the surrounding terrain.

Disrupt the Enemy

3-24. After making contact with the enemy, the company commander uses the element of surprise to conduct shaping operations to disrupt the enemy. Indirect artillery and mortar fires provide coverage throughout the initial phases of an offensive operation and the concentration of direct and indirect fires prevents the enemy from conducting and organizing a coherent defense. Overwhelming fires help disrupt the enemy's ability to conduct reconnaissance, organize a spoiling attack, effectively communicate, and plan and control his forces. Once the process of disrupting the enemy begins, it continues throughout the offensive.

Fix the Enemy

3-25. During an offensive operation, the company fixes an enemy by physically occupying terrain or dominating access in and out of area through direct and indirect fires. It may involve seizing mountain terrain that dominates the objective so that the enemy cannot resupply, reinforce, or withdraw its defenders. Depending on the tactical situation, the company may occupy positions that isolate an objective by infiltration and stealth. The commander does not allow the enemy to maneuver. Aerial and indirect fires are commonly used in mountain operations to fix an enemy force in its current positions by directly attacking enemy maneuver elements. A primary purpose in fixing the enemy is to isolate the objective and prevent the enemy from maneuvering to reinforce the targeted unit. Fixing the enemy must be done with the minimum amount of force.

Maneuver

3-26. During an offensive operation, the company deploys rapidly to deliver the assault before the enemy force can deploy or reinforce its engaged forces. The commander makes every effort to retain the initiative and prevent the enemy from stabilizing the situation by conducting violent and resolute attacks. Offensive maneuver seeks to achieve a massing of effects at the decisive point, or at several decisive points if adequate combat power is available.

Assaulting the Objective

3-27. The company's objective may be terrain- or force-oriented. Terrain-oriented objectives require the company to seize or secure a designated area. However, to gain a terrain-oriented objective often requires fighting through enemy forces. If the objective is an enemy force, an objective area may be assigned for orientation, but the company's effort is focused on the enemy's actual location. Offensive missions conducted in mountain environments are often noncontiguous operations, spread across great distances, and are force- rather than terrain-oriented. The enemy may be a stationary or moving force. Actions on the objective start when the company begins placing fires on the objective. This action usually occurs with preparatory fires while the company is still approaching the objective.

3-28. Mountain terrain has an impact on the location of the assault position. In severely restrictive terrain, the commander should consider establishing the assault position as close to the objective as possible. Long assaults across rugged terrain tire Soldiers and increase vulnerability.

3-29. The assault force must quickly and violently execute the assault to maintain momentum to deny the enemy time to organize a more determined resistance. Enemy obstacles may slow or stop forward movement. Assaulting forces must rapidly create a breach in an obstacle or redirect the flow of the assault over or around the obstacle.

3-30. After the assault, the company immediately reorients and continues the reconnaissance and surveillance effort beyond the objective to detect enemy repositioning or counterattack forces, and to look for exploitation opportunities.

Consolidation and Reorganization

3-31. Consolidation consists of actions taken to secure and strengthen the objective and defend against enemy counterattack. The unit providing the shaping effort during the assault may or may not join the assault force on the objective. Planning considerations should include unit locations, sectors of fire, forces oriented on enemy counterattack routes, and provisions to facilitate transition to follow-on operations.

3-32. Reorganization normally is conducted concurrently with consolidation and occurs as necessary to prepare the unit for follow-on operations. Detailed planning provides the company with a plan for evacuating and recovering casualties, recovering damaged equipment, providing for prisoners of war, and integrating replacement personnel. As a part of reorganization, the company prepares for enemy counterattacks, the commitment of enemy reserves, and friendly forces follow-on missions. This includes repositioning mortars to extend organic indirect fire coverage, establishing security forward of the objective, covering likely enemy avenues of approach to the objectives, and shifting indirect fire targets to beyond the objective.

Follow Through

3-33. After seizing the objective, the commander has two main alternatives that are normally based on the commander's intent: exploit success and continue the attack or terminate the offensive operation. The company transitions to other operations and executes follow-on missions as directed by the higher commander. The company develops plans for follow-on missions based on the higher headquarters' plan, the higher commander's intent, and the anticipated situation.

PLANNING AND PREPARATION

3-34. Offensive operations are planned and coordinated using available assets coupled with offensive tactics, and techniques. Commanders must often create circumstances that allow the enemy to be attacked. Mountain offensive operations can be a challenge to companies fighting an indigenous enemy on unfamiliar soil. Planning mountain offensive operations for Infantry companies uses the same sequence and planning considerations found in FM 3-21.10, The Infantry Rifle Company, coupled with tactics and techniques unique to the rugged conditions of mountain operations.

GENERAL CONSIDERATIONS

3-35. Unique planning considerations for mountain operations include—
- Movement and insertion techniques and methods that reduce the enemy's ability to observe.
- Identification of likely enemy positions and possible ambush and contact locations in the development of movement techniques, routes, and actions on contact in a compartmentalized and canalized terrain.
- Possible degraded reaction times from other ground units.
- Challenges for sustainment functions (re-supply, MEDEVAC/CASEVAC).
- Possible climate changes (weather, precipitation, wind, temperature) that can occur quickly and can be extreme.

3-36. During mission planning for mountain operations, leaders normally plan to—
- Conduct a thorough reconnaissance.
- Conduct a terrain analysis to identify company and platoon routes, likely enemy contact (based on terrain and danger areas) and primary and alternate locations to cross terrain obstacles.
- Identify a communications plan for degraded operations.
- Integrate fires to support maneuver.
- Consider use of aviation or combat vehicles for insertion or extraction.
- Enforce a proper rest plan.

3-37. In a mountain environment, the terrain normally favors the defender. Company commanders may consider conducting limited visibility operations as a means to reduce observation, increase stealth, and achieve a level of tactical surprise. With planning, detailed reconnaissance, command and control, and training, units can achieve significant tactical gains and decisive victories by exploiting limited visibility operations in mountain terrain. Imaginative and bold limited visibility operations can minimize the advantage of terrain for the defender and shift the balance of combat power to the side that can best cope with or exploit limited visibility.

WAR FIGHTING FUNCTION CONSIDERATIONS

3-38. The company commander may use warfighting functions, supported by the capabilities added by organic or attached assets from the brigade combat team (BCT) or battalion, to aid in the planning, preparing, and execution of mountain offensive operations. General considerations are mentioned here with a detailed discussion of command and control in Chapter 2, movement in Chapter 5, and intelligence, fires, protection, and sustainment in Chapter 6.

Command and Control

3-39. In mountain offensive operations, the company commander maintains command and control by positioning himself forward with the main effort and by his direct leadership at the point of attack. He locates himself where he can maintain a current and accurate picture of the company and exercise control of his elements as the attack progresses. The commander is prepared to exploit unforeseen advantages and anticipates the need or requirement to shift his effort due to success or to preserve his freedom of maneuver.

3-40. Execution of offensive mountain operations is often decentralized in nature. Companies commonly conduct operations in areas far from their parent unit and in terrain that is not easily accessible. In this type of environment, commanders control their elements both procedurally and actively, as the situation permits, while allowing junior leaders the flexibility to adapt to changing and unforeseen circumstances.

Movement and Maneuver

3-41. Movement in mountain terrain can be either dismounted, mounted, or by air. Mounted movement may include tactical or other motorized vehicles. While movements may initially involve vehicles or aircraft, ultimately Soldiers must dismount and move by foot to reach most terrain in mountain environments.

3-42. Leaders modify tactical movements in mountain terrain to accommodate terrain restrictions. Canalizing and restrictive terrain can force a unit into narrow movement routes, leaving little space for elements to spread out into typical movement formations. For ground movement to the objective, units are often limited to modified file formations on the narrow roads and trails. Route planning is essential prior to an operation. Commanders should consider the use of all available assets to assist in his evaluation of the terrain. Assets contributing information to aid in route selection may include maps, UAS acquired information, other intelligence assets and information, the use of advance elements, route reconnaissance conducted by attack reconnaissance helicopters, and information gathered from prior operations in the area.

3-43. Leaders determine and plan the use of key terrain for all offensive operations in the mountains and deny its use to the enemy. Key terrain may include a combination of terrain features that may give a marked advantage to either friendly or enemy units. Specific areas of higher elevation are often identified as key terrain while not all high ground is necessarily considered key. High ground may not be usable or accessible from either a friendly or enemy perspective. The potential use of terrain should be analyzed from an enemy perspective as well from the friendly perspective.

3-44. Movements should attempt to exploit known enemy weaknesses in their ability to detect friendly elements. For example, in some regions, the enemy has poor night vision technology. Although mounted movement during daylight is inherently safer from a terrain perspective, night driving can help reduce the chances of enemy engagements and improvised explosive device (IED) attacks. To decrease risks from both a terrain and enemy perspective, commanders should consider night movements.

Infiltration

3-45. Infiltration may be accomplished by ground or air, depending on the unique circumstances of the mission, available resources, and the ability to maintain stealth and achieve surprise. When infiltrating by air, the noise from the aircraft reduces the element of surprise but facilitates movement and concentration of forces. A suitable landing zone must be available as well to support the mission. Leaders should consider the use of multiple landing zones, to confuse the enemy as to the objective of the action.

3-46. The cover and concealment provided in mountain terrain can be exploited by companies as well as the enemy. To increase the probability of successful offensive operations, leaders use the terrain, weather, and modified movement techniques to their advantage. For example, rough unlikely routes used during limited visibility to reduce the risk of detection by the enemy can increase the element of surprise. Limited visibility can be provided by shadows or darkness as well as by climate changes including clouds or fog.

3-47. Companies may plan to use deception as part of their normal procedures while conducting offensive movement operations. If available, companies can move in conjunction with other planned operations to conceal the true nature and purpose of their mission. For example, a platoon may conceal themselves inside routine supply vehicles for movement to an unobservable dismount location.

Overwatch

3-48. Establishing an overwatch for moving units is important to mission security and success during movement and maneuver. During planning, commanders identify key terrain features that include terrain needed for establishing overwatch of a bounding force. Most often, that terrain is located at a higher elevation. To compensate for the increase in vulnerability for compressed formations, units make maximum use of multiple routes coupled with security provided by an overwatching element during movements. Overwatching elements cover potential ambush sites along the exfiltration route to guard against enemy elements moving in after a unit passes. Return routes should be planned and varied, when possible, to increase security.

Intelligence

3-49. The company commander normally obtains IPB products from the battalion, use all available information gathering assets, and use internal assets to help consolidate information and study the terrain in order to determine the enemy's strengths, weaknesses, and probable courses of action. Operations in mountain environments have seen the use of COIST to assist the commander in compiling and understanding the vast amount of information and intelligence related information available to the company. (Chapter 6 discusses these teams in more detail.) During movement, the commander should consider using assets such as UAS to recon the route, especially potential ambush sites.

3-50. Although the commander does not have complete information concerning enemy intentions for a planned offensive action, of particular concern is whether the enemy is likely to organize a defense and maintain fighting subsequent to the initial contact. The enemy, if not interested in retention of terrain, often attempts to escape. They attack forces rather than fight in order to create contact situations that are more in their favor at a later time.

Fires

3-51. A portion of the company's fire support is from mortar systems organic to the Infantry company and battalion. Other support comes from artillery and air assets. Fires are planned along the route and potential ambush sites are specifically targeted.

3-52. The commander employs supporting fires in the offense to achieve a variety of purposes which may include—

- Suppressing enemy weapons systems that inhibit movement.
- Fixing or neutralizing bypassed enemy elements.
- Preparing enemy positions for an assault. Preparatory fires are normally used during a deliberate attack, with fires placed on key targets before the assault begins. These indirect fires are integrated and synchronized with the company's direct fire plan to provide constant

pressure on the enemy position and prevent him from reacting to, or repositioning against, the company's assaulting elements. The commander weighs the benefits of preparatory fires against the potential loss of surprise.

- Obscuring enemy observation or screening friendly maneuver. The company can take advantage of smoke in various maneuver situations, such as during a bypass or in deception operations.
- Supporting breaching operations. Fires are employed to obscure and suppress the enemy that is overwatching reinforcing obstacles.
- Illuminating enemy positions. Illumination fires are included in contingency plans for night attacks and may include white light as well as infrared illumination.

3-53. The fires plan is an integral part of an offensive operation. Planned and coordinated fires are used to disrupt, destroy, fix, suppress, and neutralize the enemy. Company commanders must rely on indirect fire and air assets for unexpected additional support in mountain environments. Support from additional ground units often involves time-consuming movement to the point that it may become impractical.

Protection

3-54. A main concern in mountain environments is the protection of company personnel from the effects of the terrain and weather. Commanders should remain keenly aware of force health protection issues associated with mountain environments. Weather effects can have a severe impact on personnel and planned operations to the point that the risks to personnel may outweigh the benefits of continuing the mission. Commanders should incorporate contingencies for changing weather conditions during offensive planning.

3-55. If there is an enemy air threat, to include enemy fixed-wing aircraft and UAS, the company commander should plan for and rehearse internal passive and active air defense measures. He anticipates possible contact with enemy aircraft by templating enemy helicopter and fixed-wing air corridors and avenues of approach. Unit SOPs may dictate internal air security measures and active air defense measures.

Sustainment

3-56. Sustainment in the offense assists maneuver elements in maintaining the momentum of the attack. Sustainment functions for the company are performed by the company trains positioned as far forward as the tactical situation allows. Company trains normally remain one terrain feature out of direct fire range of the enemy behind the location of the company. In mountain environments where decentralized operations are common, the company trains locate where they can best support the platoons in the accomplishment of the company's mission.

3-57. Company offensive operations that constitute a need for resupply during the course of the mission may use a variety of transport means for delivery. These include the use of air, tactical vehicles, all terrain vehicles, and pack animals when practical.

ACTIONS ON CONTACT

3-58. In the mountains, enemy contact may be made through any of the eight forms of contact (visual, direct fire, indirect fire, obstacles, enemy or unknown aircraft, CBRN, electronic warfare, or non hostile contact) as described in FM 3-21.10, The Infantry Rifle Company. Commanders plan and prepare for actions company personnel take after any form of contact. Mountain terrain often causes a deviation from actions that are normally taken at lower elevations where maneuverability is easier and options are greater. Units plan for actions on contact that include options for maneuver based on the restrictive terrain typical in mountain environments. During movements in mountain terrain, protection from unexpected contact should be enhanced through the employment of an overwatching element.

3-59. Commanders should use all available information and intelligence to enhance operations and aid in unit protection. By planning for contact and changing the company movement technique when necessary, the commander increases his unit's protection while decreasing the enemy threat. For example, commanders that use a terrain analysis and other intelligence information to determine where and when an enemy ambush is likely to occur can avoid a surprise engagement and gain an offensive advantage.

3-60. When contact is made, leaders need to quickly analyze each contact situation to determine immediate follow-on actions. Battle drills should be well thought out and practiced in advance to reduce the amount of confusion time needed for deciding follow-on actions. Delays in taking appropriate actions unnecessarily increase risk to Soldiers. Because it is extremely important to maintain momentum in the attack, the enemy will attempt to slow or stop a friendly unit's advance by employing ambushes, obstacles and fires. By developing and refining specific battle drills and tactical standing operating procedures, units can quickly and decisively respond to enemy contact even in the most restrictive terrain.

Enemy ambush

3-61. Mountain terrain is particularly suited for emplacement of ambushes. Enemy ambush sites often include low lying areas with easily defended entry and exit locations. During movement planning for mountain operations, leaders need to pay particular attention to terrain that canalizes forces into potential enemy ambush sites. Narrow passes and valleys are often the only means to travel between locations (see Figure 3-1) without using long, indirect routes. An indigenous enemy is particularly aware of these areas and may use them to his advantage. He may observe company movements on a route used during a particular mission and emplace an ambush on the same route as the unit returns. Considerations avoiding an enemy ambush include—

- Having an overwatching unit observe friendly movements in the mountains.
- Having available artillery or air assets cover unit movements when possible. (The enemy in Afghanistan often does not emerge or fight when air assets are on station.)
- Using available reconnaissance and surveillance assets (including manned and unmanned aircraft) to reduce enemy capability of large ambushes.
- Using alternate return routes when possible.
- Avoiding routines that set patterns.
- Using noise and light discipline at night.

3-62. The best counter-ambush technique is to destroy the enemy before friendly forces are exposed in the kill zone. This requires leaders to anticipate possible ambush positions and plan their counter actions. Soldiers should be constantly alert for the enemy and any signs of enemy activity such as wires, recently disturbed earth, and movement. If an ambush site is identified, the leader can call for fires, establish support by fire positions, and maneuver against the enemy's flank and rear if possible.

3-63. While dismounted, counter-ambush actions usually consist of actions based on battle drills followed by specific actions that are quickly planned and executed. Leaders plan and rehearse counter ambush actions prior to the operation. During movement they constantly anticipate enemy contact and visualize their unit's actions on contact. Properly executed, battle drills have Soldiers seek cover, return fire, maneuver against the enemy, and allow the leader time to develop and execute a specific plan to destroy the enemy. While battle drills often involve seeking cover, returning fire, fixing, and maneuvering on the enemy, they are usually not sufficient to destroy a well-prepared enemy. In anticipating and planning his reaction to an ambush, the leader should understand that:

- Maneuver space may be limited.
- Attempting to break contact may further expose personnel.
- The terrain may restrict typical actions.

3-64. If mounted, unit actions may be even more restricted. Leaders should consider that if ambushed while mounted, the best course of action may be to return fire and break contact. The time it takes to dismount and transition the combat power to maneuvering dismounted Soldiers is often more detrimental than breaking contact. It also may expose dismounted soldiers in the kill zone. Ambushes are often initiated from a distance and from higher elevations. Dismounting and maneuvering on foot to engage the aggressors over steep difficult terrain takes time; gives the enemy a chance to escape; and may increase risk to personnel. Leaders should consider using indirect or air assets to attack the enemy as the vehicles move out of contact.

Enemy Indirect Fire

3-65. A common tactic for an enemy operating in the mountains is to attack friendly forces with indirect fires. These attacks may range from the use of mortars to large caliber artillery. The use of mortars, and sometimes light rockets, allow the enemy a long range stand-off distance from which they can engage friendly forces and then quickly leave before the unit can maneuver on them or return effective fire. To the advantage of U.S. forces, these attacks may be less accurate and less effective than friendly force indirect fires due to fire missions being shot in the direct lay mode. Many forces do not have the advantage of precision grid locations, fire direction centers, meteorological data, registration data, or the ability to stay in one place long enough to accurately adjust fires.

3-66. The enemy may tend to use the same firing positions over and over again which is both an advantage and a disadvantage. An enemy without adequate indirect fire control can fire more accurately from a previously used position. By using the same position, they can become accustomed to quickly setting up and directly aiming their fires. During mountain combat operations, mortar plates have been found cemented in place to facilitate quick set up and targeting. The disadvantage for the enemy is that friendly forces can target these areas for quick counterfire should they detect fires from those locations. Units on patrol should record, template, and report potential enemy firing positions.

3-67. While leaders determine planned reactions to enemy indirect fires, units have found one of the most effective ways to counter enemy indirect fires is to take cover, return fire to suppress them, and attack them with air assets as quickly as possible. With CAS or CCA in the air, enemy mortar fires often shut down quickly. Commanders can also attach mortar sections or squads to platoons and thus make immediately responsive fires available to the platoon leader.

OFFENSIVE TASKS

3-68. Offensive operations conducted by Infantry companies operating in mountain environments may include missions such as MTCs, attacks, special-purpose attacks, or other common activities. Company missions in higher elevation mountain terrain generally tend to be executed by dismounted platoon and squad level units. Terrain space restrictions often limit effective maneuver by larger units. While companies may conduct company level operations or operations as part of a larger force, those engagements tend to be at lower elevations where the terrain allows for their movement and maneuver.

MOVEMENT TO CONTACT

3-69. In an MTC, company elements attempt to gain contact with the enemy. The intent is to move in a way that avoids enemy detection and attack any force within the capability of the friendly unit. The two types of MTC are the approach march and the search and attack. The company normally only participates as a subelement in an approach march conducted by battalion or larger force. Generally, the company, or company elements, use the search and attack technique when conducting an MTC in mountain environments.

3-70. A search and attack is used when the enemy is operating as small, dispersed element, or when the task is to deny the enemy the ability to move within a given area. In planning a search and attack, the commander designates finding, fixing, and finishing forces. Once the enemy is located, a fixing force develops the situation and can either block potential enemy escape routes or maintains contact with the enemy. The finishing force then attacks and destroys the enemy. If conducting a search and attack on its own, the company commander must ensure coverage of all associated tasks involved in the planning, preparing, and execution of the mission. A company, or company element, conducts a search and attack to—

- Prevent the enemy from massing and organizing personnel or forces for hostile actions.
- Collect information about the enemy disposition and intent.
- Destroy or render the enemy combat ineffective.
- Prevent the enemy from operating unhindered in a given area.

3-71. Terrain that restricts friendly units to small elements will most likely restrict the enemy to sizes allowing for search and attacks to be conducted by platoon or smaller units. Units conducting a search and attack mission follow the same general guidelines as outlined in FM 3-21.10, The Infantry Rifle Company. Considerations for conducting a search and attack in the mountains include—

- Using battalion and BCT reconnaissance and surveillance assets to assist units in finding the enemy.
- Using indirect fire, air assets, or both to help fix and finish the enemy.
- Employing tactics for an enemy that may be familiar with the terrain, a hard-to-find, and usually has good observation or current intelligence of friendly movements.
- Employing sustainment solutions for resupply of lengthy search and attack missions.

Finding the Enemy

3-72. A key factor in conducting offensive operations in mountain environments is first determining where the enemy is or suspected to be. It is often difficult to locate the enemy in rugged mountain terrain that offers excellent cover and concealment for light infantry or paramilitary forces with a small vehicle, sustainment, and C2 footprint. The enemy may initiate contact when it is to his advantage or to disrupt friendly operations. Finding an enemy in such an environment often requires—

- Support from the local population or a segment of the population.
- Rapid response to intelligence.
- Operations with armed local friendly forces familiar with the terrain and people.
- Constant small-unit actions in the AO such as patrolling and ambushes.
- Use of OPs and check points.
- Manned and unmanned aerial reconnaissance and ground sensors.
- Intelligence personnel to filter, organize, and analyze data.

3-73. A reconnaissance force may be designated to assist in finding the enemy and should be a small unit able to move quickly and undetected. Reconnaissance may also include assets such as battalion and BCT reconnaissance and surveillance units, electronic signal direction finding devices, UAS, and aircraft. (For more information see Chapter 6 of this manual.)

Fixing the Enemy

3-74. Once the enemy is located and identified, the leader should determine if an engagement with the enemy is within the capability of his unit. Once that decision is made, the fixing force develops the situation and executes one of two options based on the commander's guidance and METT-TC conditions. The first option is to fix the enemy by blocking identified routes they may use to escape. The second option is to fix the enemy in his current location until the finishing force can engage him.

3-75. To fix the enemy is to decisively engage him so that he cannot maneuver and cannot escape. In mountain terrain, the defender is often aware of friendly operations and movements. Therefore, fixing a dismounted enemy can be a difficult task. The enemy can escape detection or escape being fixed in place due to the cover and concealment provided by mountain terrain, the limitations on maneuver space, and the time required for friendly maneuver. Commanders should consider the use of indirect and air assets as a means to hold the enemy in place while finishing forces maneuver to conduct the attack. Attempts to fix enemy personnel in position in order to attack them may be complicated if—

- The enemy breaks contact.
- The enemy uses stay-behind forces and long-range fires to slow and divert the attackers.
- Blocking forces cannot get in position in time.
- The enemy splits into smaller groups to break contact and escape from the area.
- Indirect fires cannot be observed.

3-76. U.S. forces usually fix the enemy by maneuvering units into blocking positions and using fires to maintain contact and to block the enemy's escape routes. Constant pressure must be applied from first contact to destruction.

Blocking Positions

3-77. A blocking position is a defensive position sited to deny the enemy access to a given area or to prevent the enemy's advance in a given direction. Units occupying these positions must be large enough and with sufficient combat power to repel any attack from the enemy. Units can use infiltration techniques or use the available cover to move and occupy the blocking position. Aerial insertion allows units to quickly occupy a position with minimal time.

3-78. Positioning blocking forces in mountain terrain by way of ground movement is difficult. It is both time consuming and tiring to the Soldier. Since defending forces may be able to observe movement, opposing forces may lose the element of surprise. If movement by ground is necessary, blocking forces should use indirect routes and cover to avoid detection.

3-79. Blocking forces may be emplaced by using air assets. Even if detected by the enemy, insertion by air is much quicker and much less exhausting. Adequate landing zones (LZs) needed for insertion can be difficult to find in the mountains and may not be ideally located. Units should avoid LZs that are too far away from the blocking position as they would negatively affect the advantages gained through surprise. Units may consider attempts of false insertions to confuse the enemy and deceive them on actual offensive operations.

3-80. Along with infiltration to the blocking position, commanders must also plan for exfiltration of the blocking force to include contingencies for exfiltration under fire if required. Commanders should also plan to shift the main effort to the blocking force if the fight is taken there by escaping enemy personnel. Shifting of indirect and air assets to support a change in the main effort should be thoroughly considered during the planning process for the operation.

3-81. A complication to the use of blocking positions in the mountains is that the terrain can allow for enemy observation of approaching units and provides exceptional avenues of egress for escaping enemy personnel. Units should be alert for evaders using dry streams, tunnels, goat trails, mountain passes and other terrain features to aid in their escape.

Direct and Indirect Fires

3-82. Both direct and indirect fires may be more effective than blocking positions in the mountains for fixing the enemy in a location. Once enemy personnel are located through contact or intelligence and offensive actions are initiated, immediate direct and indirect fires can cause enemy personnel to seek cover while friendly forces maneuver. For example, if contact is made while on patrol and follow-on offensive actions are warranted, units can use their direct fire weapons to initially fix enemy personnel followed quickly by their organic 60mm mortars fired in the direct lay, handheld mode.

3-83. Fires from the 60mm mortars are usually at the leader's discretion without clearance from higher authority. These mortar fires have proved to be greatly effective in the mountains due to their quick response time and ability to fire into unobservable areas. Infantry company commanders should consider attaching company mortars to the platoons for use in immediate responsive fires to help fix and kill enemy personnel in position.

3-84. Mortars fired in direct lay mode are quick and responsive but should quickly be followed by artillery fires if available. Every Soldier should know how to call for fire. Indirect artillery fires can greatly assist in fixing and killing enemy personnel in a combined arms offensive effort. If using artillery fires for fixing an enemy in the mountains, it is best to target avenues of egress enemy personnel are likely to use. Planned fires on these avenues can prevent enemy forces from escaping using those routes or may help channel them onto another route with a planned kill zone.

3-85. If available, other weapons systems such as the Javelin and the ITAS can be used. These systems can be used for long range engagements of targets in fortified or heavily protected positions. These systems are often employed where some means of transportation other than foot Soldiers is available for moving the equipment.

3-86. Commanders should consider employing specially-trained small units, such as sniper teams to infiltrate the AO prior to the attack to provide direct observation. They can also call for and adjust indirect fires and provide long-range direct fires.

Finishing the Enemy

3-87. In the mountains, the finishing forces often include the use of all available assets including direct fire, indirect fire, and fires supplied by air assets. Ground and air observation of possible escape routes should be maintained as well as direct coordination between all ground and air assets to facilitate a quick response to enemy reactions.

HASTY AND DELIBERATE ATTACKS

3-88. As with most mountain operations, conducting a hasty or deliberate attack can be more difficult than one conducted on less restrictive terrain. As elevation increases, mountain terrain and climate become increasingly restrictive on planning and executing attacks. The mountain environment commonly favors the defender and limits the key element of surprise for the attacker. Positioning of a blocking force can also be difficult or impossible, requiring other alternatives to contain the enemy. Accordingly, attacks must be carefully planned, coordinated, and executed in order to achieve the desired effect. (Figure 3-1.)

3-89. Company deliberate attacks involve the following:
- UAS identifies enemy forces in the company AO.
- Company commander decides to conduct an attack to seize OBJ MARK.
- Lift and attack helicopters refuel at FARP and move from PZ JAKE.
- 3rd platoon air assaults into a blocking position in vicinity of LZ PETE.
- 1st platoon establishes SBF DAN on hill overlooking OBJ MARK.
- 2nd platoon conducts road movement to dismount point and occupies ATK position SAM.
- Indirect assets fire preparation fires on OBJ MARK.
- 2nd platoon on order attacks northeast to seize OBJ MARK.
- CCA destroys enemy withdrawing into EA JIM.

3-90. Attacks are characterized by speed, flexibility, and surprise. Restrictive mountain terrain limits the advantages of the attacking force, driving commanders to conduct deliberate as opposed to hasty attacks in the mountains. The increased time allows for careful planning, preparation, and coordination of all aspects of the attack including fire planning, use of air assets, route planning, and C2.

3-91. Unique considerations for planning attacks in mountain environments include the—
- Use of terrain and weather by friendly and enemy units.
- Negotiation of obstacles.
- Use of supporting assets.

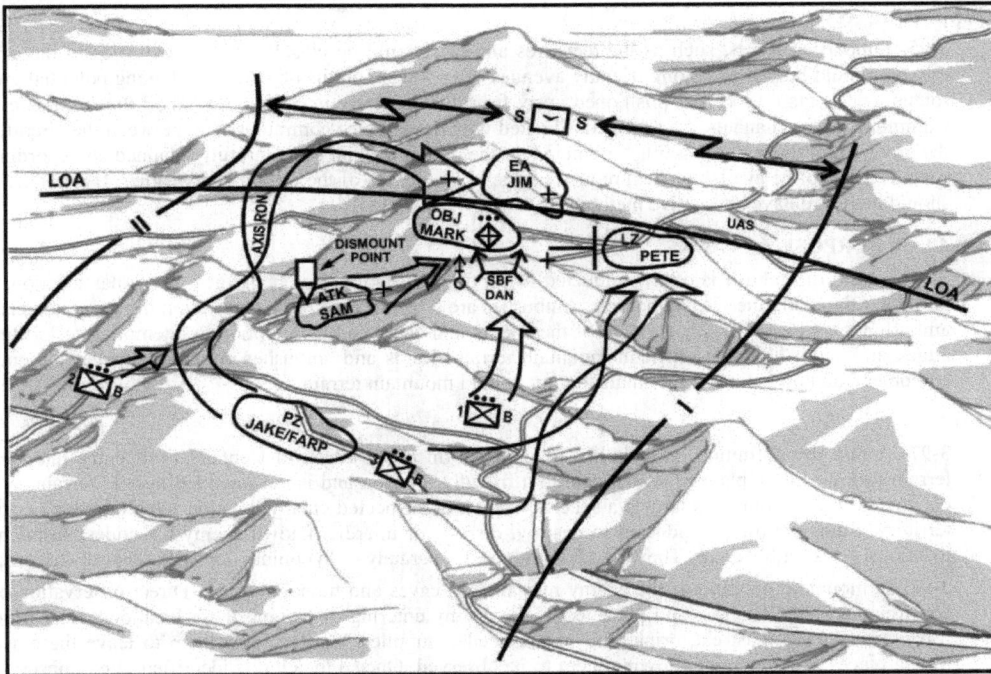

Figure 3-1. Deliberate attack

Terrain and Weather

3-92. When planning an attack, commanders view the terrain from an enemy perspective. In mountain environments, the enemy generally will attempt to control terrain that denies the attacker avenues of approach such as roads, trail networks, valleys, dry stream beds, and other less restrictive terrain. To control these areas the enemy seeks control of key terrain in the surrounding high ground including ridgelines, hills, peaks, and rock formations where, if occupied, they can influence operations. Leaders should analyze the terrain and plan to deny these areas to the enemy in their scheme of maneuver.

3-93. Taking advantage of the terrain and weather conditions is critical in mountain operations for U.S. forces. Without their use, the enemy is routinely aware of friendly force movements. Mountain weather conditions, such as overcast conditions or fog, can be effectively used to the company's advantage while conducting an attack. Terrain features also aid in covering and concealing friendly movements. Movement through unobservable terrain such as dense vegetation, rock formations, and depressions limits observation. Movement in rough terrain during limited visibility conditions slows movement rates and increases the risk of Soldier injury from trips and falls. Some limited visibility conditions may also affect air and other assets.

Natural and Man-Made Obstacles

3-94. A careful analysis of potential obstacles can be conducted during the planning process for an attack. The attacking force should be able to move quickly and unobstructed to the objective. A simple map reconnaissance is often not adequate as some features that are extremely difficult to negotiate in mountain terrain may be barely visible on a map. Information gained from ground and air reconnaissance coupled with information from units or personnel that previously traversed the area can help in identifying obstacles. If an obstacle cannot be quickly negotiated, alternate routes to the objective must be found or assets provided to cross or breach the obstacle.

Supporting Assets

3-95. Supporting assets, such as indirect fires and air, should be closely coordinated prior to the attack. Targets should be planned along friendly avenues of approach, on the objective, and along potential escape routes. Air assets may be pre-positioned away from the objective in order not to spoil the surprise effect. Communications channels should be coordinated with direct voice communication between the aircraft and the ground unit during the assault. Commanders should realize that even carefully planned and coordinated support may not be available when requested due to the effects of the terrain and weather. If possible, they should therefore have alternative methods on-hand.

SPECIAL-PURPOSE ATTACKS

3-96. A raid or ambush is often conducted to capture or destroy the enemy at a particular location, at a particular time, and then leave the area. Ambushes are a common offensive operation in the mountains. An ambush allows for covert observation of the enemy and can be a viable option to attempting to locate and attack an enemy hiding in difficult mountain terrain. Raids and ambushes commonly target the enemy, equipment, and operations rather than attempt to hold mountain terrain.

Raid

3-97. A raid, by definition, is a limited-objective form of an attack that entails swift entry into hostile terrain followed by a planned withdrawal to a friendly location and is not intended to hold terrain. A raid conducted in the mountains targets a specific known or suspected enemy location within enemy occupied territory. Raids are often conducted to destroy, disrupt, or interdict known enemy C2 nodes, sustainment locations, or assembly areas. They may be conducted separately or in conjunction with other operations.

3-98. In mountain operations, the enemy may hide in caves and tunnel systems. Direct observation often confirms the exact location and presence of the enemy entering or leaving these locations. Like friendly forces, the enemy must eat, drink, and obtain needed supplies. This requires them to leave these secure hiding places at some point allowing them to be observed. Once a location is identified, direct observation should confirm the best time for the raid to be conducted on the position. Observation can help determine time patterns and enemy strengths.

3-99. Leaders should consider the unique aspects of conducting a raid in the mountains and be cautious while planning the withdrawal of friendly forces at the conclusion of the operation. Primary and alternate withdrawal routes and means of extraction should be carefully planned in order to protect friendly forces from counterattack and ambush.

Ambush

3-100. An ambush initiated by friendly forces in mountain terrain is conducted using the same procedures and METT-TC analysis as in any other location. In the same manner as friendly forces, the restrictive terrain often confines the enemy to habitual paths such as roads, trails, and foot paths. Direct observation and intelligence can indicate where and when the enemy is likely to travel so a suitable ambush location can be identified.

3-101. Key to establishing an effective ambush in the mountains is covert movement to the ambush site. The use of limited visibility conditions can aid in covering these movements. Another technique to consider for disguising movement to an ambush site is by using a stay-behind ambush. Assuming the enemy is monitoring all movement, vehicles that normally carry one squad or carry supplies can be loaded with an extra squad to be used in the ambush. At some point during the movement, the ambush squad dismounts in an unobservable manner while the other continues with a separate mission or returns to base. Planners should look for terrain characteristics such as high ground above a potential ambush site. Along with other considerations such as adequate clear fields of fire into the kill zone, leaders should capitalize on the increased advantages the terrain offers. Often, in lower elevations, crossing fires between friendly units may result in fratricide. In the mountains, it is often possible to avoid potential danger from friendly crossing fires by positioning personnel on high ground elevations on both sides of the kill zone.

3-102. Leaders should also consider the use of an ambush as part of a defense plan for a unit location if the availability of personnel supports their use. An ambush that employs the use of items such as command detonated claymore mines may require fewer personnel. This type of ambush may be an alternative if personnel strength is limited.

Chapter 4

Defensive Operations

While U.S. operations are inherently offensive in nature, defensive operations are necessary in order to support offensive operations, or for protection or security as designated by the unit's mission. Commanders should remember that enemy actions may range from major unit attacks as were encountered during the Korean War at Pork Chop Hill or Combat Outpost Keating in Afghanistan to limited assaults or harassing fires typical during stability operations.

REFERENCES

4-1.   Table 4-1 consolidates the references to additional information.

Table 4-1. Guide for subjects referenced in text

Subject	References
Operations	FM 3-0
Tactics	FM 3-90
The Infantry Battalion	FM 3-21.20
The Infantry Rifle Company	FM 3-21.10

OVERVIEW

4-2.   Defensive operations in the mountains are conducted to resist, defeat, or destroy an enemy attack in order to support subsequent offensive operations. Commanders use defensive operations to withstand an enemy attack while preparing to seize the initiative and develop conditions favorable for transitioning to offensive operations. During a defense, friendly forces withstand enemy attacks and hold the enemy while preparing to seize the initiative and transition to an attack or to conduct stability tasks. A thorough understanding of the commander's intent is especially critical in defensive operations, which demand precise integration of all assets including combat and sustainment.

4-3.   U.S. forces operating in mountain environments often possess weapons and equipment more advanced in technology than the enemy. Knowing this, enemy offensive tactics commonly involve short violent engagements followed by a hasty withdrawal through preplanned routes. They often strike quickly and fight only as long as the advantage of the initial surprise is in their favor. Attacks may include direct fires, indirect fires, or IEDs and may be against stationary or moving forces.

CHARACTERISTICS

4-4.   The characteristics of the defensive operations for the Infantry company include preparation, security, disruption, massing effects, flexibility, and maneuver.

Preparation

4-5.   In noncontiguous mountain operations, companies often defend from a strongpoint or battle position. A perimeter defensive plan is commonly established and coordinated with all available assets. Preparations for the defense do not cease but rather improvements continue and plans refined for the entire time the company or company element is in position. Commanders take advantage of the available time to conduct thorough preparations for a defense. Through the proper selection of terrain and reinforcing obstacles, units can direct the energy of the enemy's attack into terrain of their own choosing. Preparation of the ground consists of plans for fires and movement and counterattack plans. It also includes preparation of positions, routes, obstacles, logistics, and command and control facilities.

Security

4-6.   Security efforts in mountain environments depend largely on early warnings of pending enemy actions in order to allow reaction time for the company commander. Security actions assist in inhibiting and defeating enemy operations. Observation posts, patrols, sensors, aerial platforms, and other assets aid in providing security for company operations.

Disruption

4-7.   Defensive plans aim at disrupting the enemy's planned operations and upsetting his tempo and synchronization. Counterattacks, indirect fires, obstacles, and retention of key or decisive terrain prevent the enemy from concentrating his strength against portions of the defense. Well-coordinated defense plans assist in early disruption of enemy offensive actions.

Massed Effects

4-8.   The concentration of combat power at the decisive time and place is key to a successful defense. In the mountains, defensive operations are often area defenses conducted from battle positions and strongpoints where the retention of terrain is critical. To support these types of defenses, company commanders integrate the massing of combat power in their defensive plans. Massing effects include the use of air, indirect and direct fires that can shift to critical points rapidly to provide destructive effects, such as targeted final protective fires. Massing effects requires effective command and control with redundancy in communications, and engagement criteria for artillery, mortars, air assets, and crew served weapons.

Flexibility

4-9.   The company commander considers establishing a defensive plan that centers on the most likely offensive actions the enemy will take. He also builds in flexibility in order to shift the main effort if required. He provides for flexibility through the use of supplementary positions, reserves, and counter attack plans. In the mountains, an analysis of how the enemy may use mountain terrain in the offensive allows the commander to anticipate enemy actions and prepare flexible contingencies.

Maneuver

4-10. Maneuver allows the company commander to use the terrain to support movement in combination with fire to support the defensive operation. In the mountains, maneuver space is often limited depending on where the defense is located. Commanders include these limitations in their defensive plans while still using available maneuver space to his advantage.

TYPES

4-11. The company may conduct defensive operations on their own or participate in a larger battalion or higher level defense. During the conduct of these operations the company may defend, delay, withdraw, counterattack, or perform security tasks. (For further detail on these operations see FM 3-21.20 and FM 3-90.) The three types of defensive operations the company may be involved in are the following:

- Area defense. Concentrates on denying the enemy access to designated terrain for a specified time, rather than the outright destruction of the enemy. Units at all echelons may conduct an area defense.
- Mobile defense. Orients on the destruction of the enemy through a decisive attack(s) by a striking force. In the mountains where maneuver space is limited, a mobile defense is conducted by division and larger units and can be difficult to synchronize.
- Retrograde Operations. Forces or voluntary organizes movements to the company support area or away from the enemy and is part of a larger scheme of maneuver.

4-12. Unless participating in a planned defensive operation conducted at battalion level or higher, Infantry company defensive operations in mountain environments will normally be perimeter or strongpoint area defenses established on a specific piece of terrain.

PLANNING AND PREPARATION

4-13. Defensive operations are planned and coordinated using available assets in a synchronized and coordinated defensive plan. Planning mountain defensive operations for Infantry companies uses the same planning considerations found in FM 3-21.10 coupled with tactics and techniques unique to the rugged conditions of mountain operations.

GENERAL CONSIDERATIONS

4-14. Unique planning considerations for mountain defensive operations include—

- Defensive plans for a 360-degree perimeter defense in a noncontiguous mountain environment.
- Enemy avenues of approach through canalized terrain, typically dismounted.
- Economy of force considerations along unlikely enemy avenues of approach (i.e. terrain features too difficult to negotiate without considerable time and equipment).
- Noncontiguous operations without mutual supporting direct fires with adjacent units.
- Use of air and indirect fires to support the defensive plan.
- Employment of engineer assets to aid in position construction to increase survivability and protection and to emplace shaping obstacles along enemy avenues of approach.

4-15. During establishment of a defensive position in the mountains, the following priority-of-work areas need to be considered. (For complete coverage of priority-of work areas, see FM 3-21.10.)

- Key Weapons Positions. Careful selection of key weapons positions should cover likely mounted and dismounted avenues of approach. Antiarmor weapons require adequate space and ventilation for backblast and cover vehicular trafficable avenues while machine guns (MGs) and squad automatic weapons (SAWs) cover dismounted avenues of approach. Place weapons near ground level if possible to increase grazing fires. Weapons should be mutually supporting.
- Fields of fire. Ensuring clear fields of fire may sometimes be a challenge in mountain environments. Loopholes, aiming stakes, sector stakes, and target reference points can help in target engagements. Commanders need to plan coverage for unobservable dead space.
- Avenues of Approach. Identify and secure avenues of approach, including subsurface avenues. Main avenues in mountain terrain are often clearly identifiable but considerations must be given to less likely difficult avenues as well.
- Stockpiling of Supplies and Equipment. Depending on the type of defensive operation, stockpiling ammunition, food, drinking water, medical supplies, and fire-fighting equipment may be required.
- Barriers and Obstacles. Commanders should consider construction of barriers and emplacement of obstacles to deny enemy access. Integrate barriers and obstacles with key weapons and cover observation and fire (both direct and indirect). Barriers and obstacles are comprised of two types, natural (such as mountains, thick vegetation, streams, gullies, and cliffs) and man-made (fences, walls, gates, vehicle barriers, wire, mines, and other items). If possible, conceal obstacles from enemy observation, erect an irregular pattern to hinder enemy movement, employ in depth, and tie-in with existing obstacles.
- Routes. Movement routes between positions should be improved and marked if possible as well as the routes to alternate and supplementary positions. In mountain terrain, this may require emplacing special equipment such as ropes for climbing and rappelling.
- Security positions. Key positions for OPs and other surveillance assets should be established to ensure observation of enemy avenues of approach.
- Other assets. Other assets may be coordinated and integrated into the overall defensive plan including indirect fire assets and aviation assets including the use of UAS.

WARFIGHTING FUNCTION CONSIDERATIONS

4-16. The company commander may use warfighting functions to aid in the planning, preparing, and execution of mountain defensive operations. General considerations are mentioned here with a detailed discussion of command and control in Chapter 2, movement in Chapter 5, and intelligence, fires, protection, and sustainment in Chapter 6.

Command and Control

4-17. Commanders establish defensive plans and control measures for effective command and control during defensive operations. Plans should be well rehearsed with all subordinate units and personnel clear on assigned duties and areas of responsibility. Typical defensive positions in mountain environments involve 360-degree perimeter defensive plans. Defensive plans are established with ample flexibility to allow the commander to shift assets in response to enemy actions and reactions to contain the enemy's attack.

Movement and Maneuver

4-18. Mountain terrain plays a major role in determining how a unit defends. Movement corridors, or terrain where movement is more common and less restrictive, are often easily identified by friendly and enemy units. Mountain terrain often restricts maneuver to identifiable locations and restricts movement by lengthening the time it takes to traverse a particular piece of ground. Considerations for employment of movement and maneuver in mountain environments may include—
- Planning for a terrain rather than an enemy oriented defense of a static position aimed at slowing, disrupting, and stopping enemy attacks before their final assault.
- Planning for canalized, restricted maneuver space when identifying primary, alternate, supplementary, and subsequent positions during a defense using battle positions.
- Defensive planning staged around positions the company intends to hold such as forward operating bases and combat outposts or other bases.
- Effective weapons positioning within the position and on key mountain terrain features that offer good flanking fires on an attacking force.

Intelligence

4-19. In developing defensive plans, the commander uses a variety of IPB products from the battalion as well as local information sources to identify probable enemy actions and avenues of approach. COISTs can help commanders sift through intelligence and information in order to understand how, when, and where enemy attacks may occur. The COIST helps the commander maintain situational awareness, supporting targeting, and supporting passing the commander's information requirement to subordinate units.

Fires

4-20. Company commanders plan integration of available fires into the defensive plan. Coordinated fires from indirect and air systems are essential in defensive operations in mountain environments as support from reinforcing ground units may come from some distance away. Preplanned fires from internal and external indirect fire assets can help deliver an initial blow to an enemy attack while air assets are in route to assist. Air and indirect fires should be synchronized with, direct fires, obstacles, and counter attack plans.

Protection

4-21. Commanders consider the use of protection measures from direct fires, indirect fires, and air attack while establishing defensive plans. In mountain environments, establishment of some of these protection measures often call for the use of external assets for many positions. Engineers are often needed to assist in the emplacement of obstacles and to dig in or build up a position. It is extremely difficult to dig into rocky mountain terrain and protection. Building up a position rather than digging it in often improves protection. In mountain environments where defensive operations are often associated with established bases such as combat outposts, heavy equipment is commonly used to build walls and overhead protection.

4-22. Protection from air attacks by air defense assets focus on likely air avenues of approach for enemy aircraft. They can provide area coverage in and around a defensive position. Air avenues of approach tend to be more restrictive in mountain environments. Mountain ridges may be too high for aircraft to cross requiring approaches that more closely correspond to the enemy's ground avenues of approach. Mountain ranges also aid in protection from a rear approach of a unit oriented toward a valley or depression. Considerations should include possible LZs enemy aircraft may use. Units should always consider the use of both passive and active air defense measures to aid in protection.

Sustainment

4-23. Sustainment considerations for defensive operations in mountain environments are similar to those for the offense. Commanders may consider stockpiling of supplies and ammunition to support engagements where resupply may be hindered. Procedures for the care and evacuation of wounded personnel while conducting a defense should be included in the defensive plan. (See Chapter 6 for more information.)

AREA DEFENSE

4-24. The area defense is a type of defensive operations that concentrates on denying enemy forces access to designated terrain for a specific time rather than destroying the enemy outright (FM 3-0). Infantry companies conducting mountain operations are often directed to conduct this type of defense around established positions such as a base of operations or a key piece of terrain. The dominating hills, ridges, and peaks of mountain terrain are ideally suited for defensive operations. Units occupying strong points located on dominating heights can defend their own position and help control passes and lines of communication in surrounding areas.

DEFENSIVE TECHNIQUES

4-25. When the situation dictates a dispersion of units in mountain environments, the planning for a 360-degree defense is often required for most positions occupied. Companies often operate out of established positions or bases such as combat outposts and conduct defensive or security operations in the areas of these bases. Attacks on these positions may be a direct assault, come in the form of indirect fire, or a combination of both. Enemy engagements may be short and their fires inaccurate depending on the weapons used, their skill, and the time involved in the attack. Enemy tactics in mountain environments may include an attack from a distance from covertly set up direct and indirect assets such as MGs, rockets, and mortars.

4-26. In planning an area defense in mountain environments, company commanders consider the characteristics of the defense along with the specific defensive technique he plans to use. Preparation for the defense continues as long as the unit is in position. Often the company or elements of the company defend an area using one of the following techniques:
- Perimeter.
- Strongpoint.
- Battle Position.
- Reverse Slope.

4-27. While other techniques are possible in mountain environments, the terrain at higher levels often limits their use due to mobility restrictions and the complicated terrain. (For information on other techniques see FM 3-21.10.)

Perimeter

4-28. A perimeter defense is a technique in which the defending force is oriented in all directions (Figure 4-1). An Infantry company conducting operations in mountain environments may be required to execute a perimeter defense under a variety of conditions, including—
- When it must hold critical terrain in areas where the defense is not tied in with adjacent units.
- When it has been bypassed and isolated by the enemy and must defend in place.
- When it conducts occupation of an independent assembly area or reserve position.
- When it begins preparation of a strongpoint.
- When it is directed to concentrate fires into two or more adjacent avenues of approach.

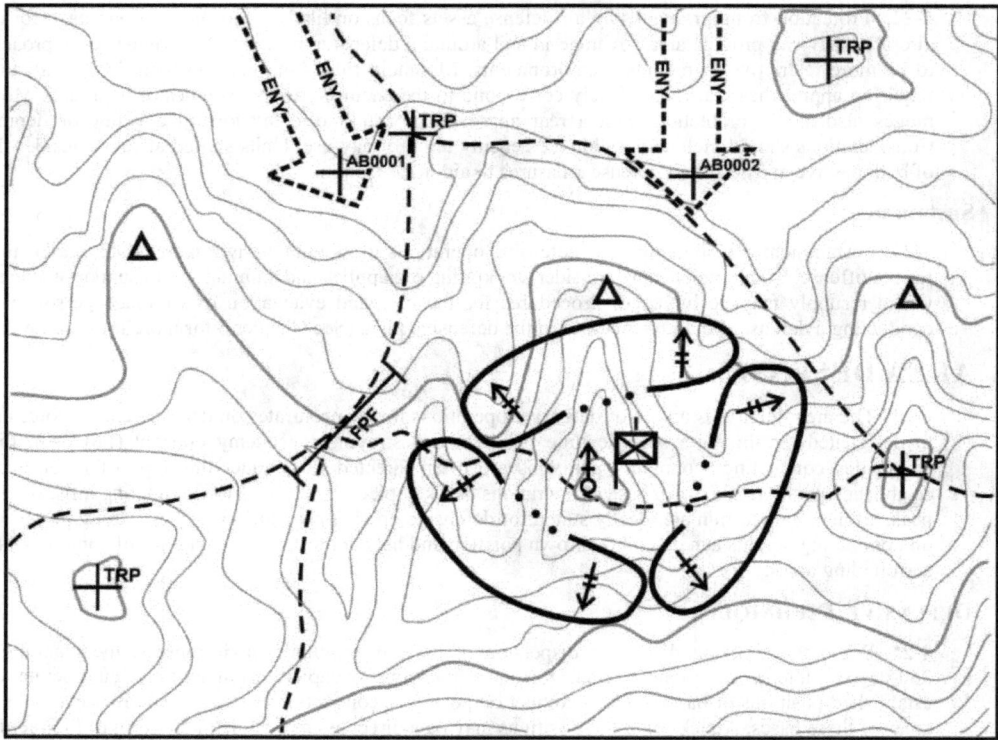

Figure 4-1. Perimeter defense

4-29. The Infantry company prepares a perimeter defense when there are no friendly units adjacent to it. Considerations for preparing a perimeter defense include—

- All-around security and defense in all directions.
- Coverage of the most likely avenues of approach.
- Alternate and supplementary positions within the perimeter.
- Placement of close combat missiles (CCMs) on possible mounted avenues of approach and snipers to observe or overwatch key areas.
- Mortar positions near the center of the perimeter so their minimum range does not restrict the ability to fire in any direction.
- Dug in and covered ammunition storage bunkers.
- Reserve of one or more rifle squads in reserve with primary positions near the most dangerous avenue of approach and supplementary positions for fighting in all directions.
- Use of obstacles in depth around the perimeter.
- Integration of direct fires, indirect fires, and air assets.
- Sustainment solutions for an extended perimeter defense including the use of air assets and landing zones for resupply and evacuation of wounded.

Strongpoint

4-30. Strongpoint positions in mountain terrain are characterized by the emplacement of direct fire weapons for all-around protection. While a series of strongpoints can provide an effective defense for a specified area, a contiguous defense in mountain terrain is not generally possible due to terrain restrictions and manpower constraints. In mountain environments, reserve forces should be close to defensive locations to offset terrain restrictions that can delay reaction times. Air support and indirect fire assets are typically integrated into the defensive plan. Around-the-clock observation, along with patrols and electronic sensors, are commonly required to counter the unique opportunities mountain terrain offers for enemy infiltration.

4-31. In mountain environments, companies are often directed to construct a strongpoint. In order to do so, companies generally augment with engineer support, additional weapons, and sustainment resources. If attacked, Soldiers defend a strongpoint until the commander directing the defense formally orders the unit out of it. The specific positioning of units in the strongpoint depends on the company commander's mission analysis. In preparing a strongpoint defense, the same considerations for a perimeter defense apply, in addition to the following:

- Reinforce each individual fighting position (to include alternate and supplementary positions) to withstand small arms fire, mortar fire, and artillery fragmentation. Stockpile food, water, ammunition, pioneer tools, and medical supplies in each fighting position.
- Support each individual fighting position with several others. Plan or construct covered and concealed routes between positions and along routes of supply and communication. Use these to support counterattack and maneuver within the strongpoint.
- Divide the strongpoint into several independent, but mutually supporting positions or sectors. If one of the positions or sectors must be evacuated or is overrun, limit the enemy penetration with obstacles and fires, and support a counterattack.
- Construct obstacles and minefields to disrupt and canalize enemy formations, to reinforce fires, and to protect the strongpoint from the assault. Place the obstacles and mines out as far as friendly units can observe them, within the strongpoint, and at points in between where they will be useful.
- Identify primary and alternate LZs for the movement of personnel and supplies when necessary. The primary LZ should be within the strongpoint itself with the alternate nearby and procedures for obtaining quick access through friendly constructed obstacles to the LZ.
- Prepare range cards for each position and confirm them by fires. Plan indirect fires in detail and register them. Also, plan indirect fires for firing directly on the strongpoint using proximity fuzes.
- Plan and test several means of communication within the strongpoint and to higher headquarters; possibilities include radio, wire, messenger, pyrotechnics, and other signals.
- Improve or repair the strongpoint until the unit is relieved or withdrawn. More positions can be built, tunnels and trenches dug, existing positions improved or repaired, and barriers built or fixed.

4-32. Strongpoints might be part of any defensive plan and are commonly established to protect vital unit operational areas, bases and key terrain. In mountain environments, strongpoints may be molded to the terrain by integrating natural camouflage and obstacles. Existing natural obstacles found in mountain terrain can support formidable strongpoints (Figure 4-2).

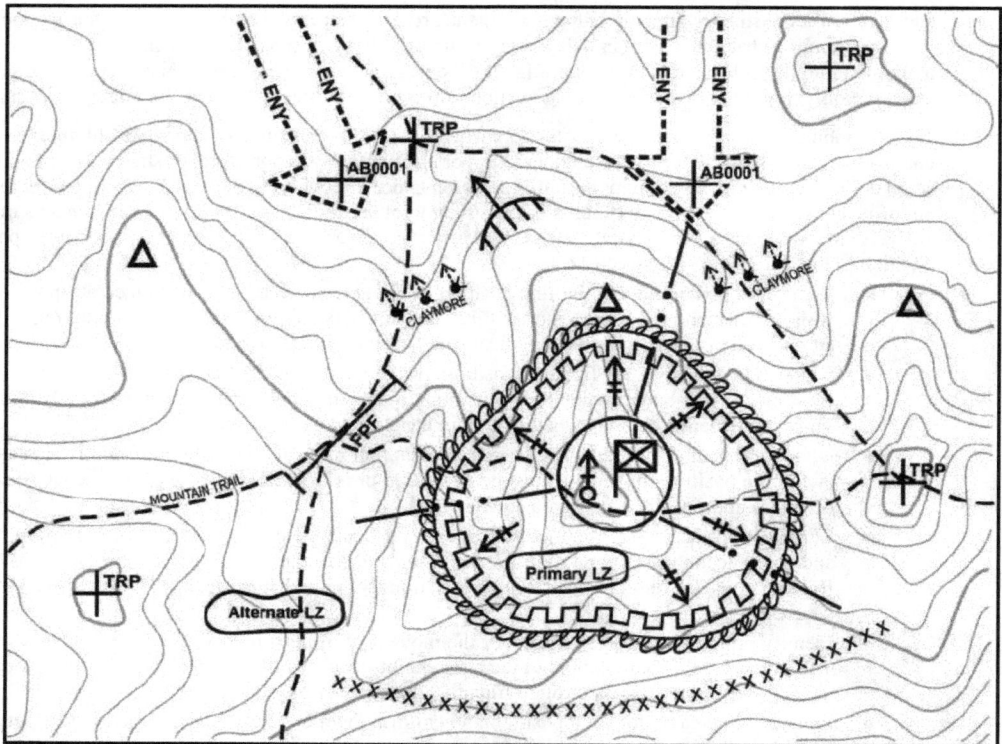

Figure 4-2. Strongpoint defense

4-33. A strongpoint defense is commonly set up to support a company combat outpost in mountain environments. A combat outpost is a defensive position that supports internal and external operations and should provide the ability to secure itself. As with other defensive positions, the challenge is to retain the initiative during an enemy attack in order to keep the enemy reacting and unable to execute his own plan. In preparation for the defense of a combat outpost, security measures should be made strong enough to halt an attack by a force significantly larger than the defending force. (For more information on combat outposts see Chapter 5.)

4-34. To reduce the risks and effects of an enemy attack, defensive plans should aim to keep the enemy ground forces as far away from the position as possible. Maximum standoff should be a consideration when leaders are deciding where to locate a strongpoint. Security patrols may also be used to assist in covering dead space and other unobservable areas. Security patrols seek to make contact with enemy elements to disrupt their operations and keep them from forming effective offensive operations against the friendly position. (For more on patrolling operations see chapter 5 of this manual.)

Battle Position

4-35. A battle position is a general location on the ground from where forces plan to defend. The company commander designates primary, alternate, supplementary, and subsequent battle positions to subordinate platoons after determining defensive engagement areas and sectors of fire.

4-36. In mountain environments the terrain may restrict occupation of a designated position determined by a means other than an onsite reconnaissance, such as a map reconnaissance. Actual locations of suitable positions are further determined after an onsite ground reconnaissance. The four types of battle positions as described in FM 3-21.10 are:

- Primary. A primary position is the position that covers the enemy's most likely avenue of approach into the AO. It is the best position to accomplish the assigned mission.
- Alternate. An alternate position is a defensive position for occupation when the primary position becomes untenable or unsuitable for carrying out the assigned task.
- Supplementary. A supplementary position is a defensive position that provides the best sectors of fire and defensive terrain along an avenue of approach that is not the primary avenue where the enemy is expected to attack.
- Subsequent. A subsequent position is a position, or series of positions, that a unit expects to move to during the course of a battle.

4-37. Mountain terrain often prevents platoons defending from battle positions from being physically tied in with adjacent units. This increases the requirement for all-around perimeter security. Platoons move from their primary, alternate, supplementary, or subsequent position only with the commander's approval, or when the commander has prescribed a particular condition as a reason to move.

Reverse Slope

4-38. Mountain operations may provide opportunities for conducting a reverse slope defense. In a reverse slope defense, the company is deployed on terrain that is masked from long range enemy direct fire and ground observation by the crest of a hill. Although some units and weapons might be positioned on the forward slope, the crest, or the counterslope (a forward slope of a hill to the rear of a reverse slope), most forces are on the reverse slope.

4-39. The key to the reverse slope defense is control of the crest of the hill. The intent is to draw the enemy onto the crest of the hill where they can be engaged with direct fire. Enemy forces that have not yet reached the crest of the hill are unable to engage in the battle effectively. This technique allows for a smaller friendly force to effectively defend against a larger enemy force by limiting the number of enemy personnel that can engage at any given time.

4-40. Advantages for using a reverse slope defense when possible include—

- Protection from long range enemy direct fire.
- Reduced enemy observation affects his ability to adjust indirect fire.
- Reduced ability for additional enemy units to support his assault.
- Deception, which may cause the enemy to advance to close contact before discovering the defensive position.
- Obstacles and clear fields of fire can be emplaced without disclosing friendly positions.
- Enemy target acquisition and jamming efforts are degraded.
- Enemy aircraft must attack from the flank or from the rear.
- Counterattacking forces have greater freedom of maneuver.

4-41. Considerations for preparing a reverse slope defense include—

- Positioning OPs forward of the crest to provide early warning and long range observation.
- Planning egress routes from the reverse slope to alternate or subsequent positions.
- Using existing natural obstacles in conjunction with emplaced obstacles to channel and contain the enemy.
- Positioning obstacles on the near side of the crest that can stall enemy forces in an engagement area and limiting his ability to assault downhill.
- Positioning weapons and assets for a close range fight.
- Positioning of reserve forces for flexibility to include considerations of counterslope positions.
- Planning and integration of indirect and air assets.
- Planning offensive counter attacks.

This page intentionally left blank.

Chapter 5

Other Tactical Operations

Infantry company commanders conduct a variety of other tactical operations in support of offensive, defensive, and other full spectrum operations in mountain environments. Common operations for mountain environments include movement, patrols, establishment of observation posts and combat outposts, air assault operations, and tunnel and cave operations. These operations help establish conditions for the successful accomplishment of critical tasks during mountain operations.

REFERENCES

5-1.   Table 5-1 consolidates the references to additional information.

Table 5-1. Guide for subjects referenced in text

Subject	References
The Infantry Rifle Platoon and Squad	FM 3-21.8
The Infantry Rifle Company	FM 3-21.10
Engineer Reconnaissance	FM 3-34.170
Military Mountaineering	FM 3-97.61
Air Assault Operations	ATTP 3-18.12

MOVEMENT

5-2.   The upper levels of mountain terrain commonly consist of barren rocky slopes sparsely sprinkled with trees and stunted bushes. Rock formations can be steep, craggy, jagged, and unforgiving. High altitude, rocky terrain with varying degrees of constantly changing slopes is an obstacle that must be continually negotiated while conducting operations in mountain environments. Mountain peaks may have little or no vegetation and can be permanently snow-covered. Further down mountain slopes vegetation commonly becomes thicker while washes, streams, rocks, and changing terrain features can remain significant obstacles. Movement is difficult at best in these conditions.

5-3.   In most cases mountain terrain severely limits mounted (and often dismounted) movement to roads and trails. The local populace and animals often create a series of trails that crisscross the mountain terrain. In many cases, ground travel to the top of a mountain requires the use of these trails for at least part of the ascent. Trails typically follow contour lines with multiple switchbacks. A straight line distance from point to point may be relatively short while actual trail distance may be lengthy. Movements are often confined to file type formations with the trails and dry stream beds becoming likely avenues of approach.

GENERAL PLANNING CONSIDERATIONS

5-4.   Planning ground movements in mountain environments includes considerations for—
- Increased time needed to traverse rough mountain terrain.
- Challenging movement between natural corridors and compartments created in mountain terrain.
- Flooding that can make travel through normally dry stream beds impossible.
- Movement through depressions and gullies that can create conditions for an enemy ambush.

- Precipitation that can have an impact on planned mobility. Dirt mountain roads without culverts or other protections against erosion can become badly damaged with ruts becoming permanent fixtures as they dry. Mountain water runoff can wash away portions roads and trails making it impassable for vehicular traffic. Roads may tend to shift over time as local personnel find routes around these washes.
- Sudden flooding that may occur in larger mountain and valley streams that are fed by mountain water runoff, streams and springs. A rain storm from miles away can cause a sudden flood in a dry stream bed used for planned movement.
- Rope systems and other specialized equipment or training that may be required to assist in mountain stream crossings or in moving up or down steep inclines.
- Snow conditions that can aid travel by covering rough terrain with a consistent surface or deep snow that can impede movement. Snowshoes, skis, and over-snow vehicles may be required.
- Avalanches that may block a planned route and remain a risk for movement in or near potential avalanche areas.
- Special training and equipment for movement across glaciers.

EFFECTS ON VEHICLE MOVEMENT

5-5. In mountain environments there is often a primitive, degraded, or canalizing road network. Constructed roads may be in a state of disrepair making vehicle traffic difficult (Figure 5-1). Roads may consist of pot-hole-riddled dirt trails barely wide enough for vehicles to pass while some of the larger, more improved, heavily traveled roads and road networks may be damaged from either old or recent military activity. Previously damaged or destroyed bridges may have been repaired while others remain broken. Trafficable roads in these environments may be few.

Figure 5-1. Mountain road

Vehicle Movement Planning Considerations

5-6.   As mountain slopes begins to rise, the ability to maneuver vehicles decreases. Mountain terrain often limits tactical movement by vehicles to a file that is almost exclusively restricted to improved or unimproved roads. Additional vehicle formations and maneuver is more easily accomplished near the base of a mountain. During movement planning, commanders should consider the risks of being confined to a vehicle, in a file, on roads used for vehicular traffic.

5-7.   The potential for an enemy ambush in mountain terrain can be a significant risk during vehicular movements. Commanders should establish react to ambush drills and standing operating procedures (SOPs) for units moving in mountain terrain where maneuver space is limited. SOPs should include actions needed to move or remove disabled vehicles blocking routes into and out of an ambush site. Enemy ambush tactics often include using terrain that channels friendly units into areas where movement is restricted, then disabling the front and/or rear vehicles to confine the unit to a kill zone. The surrounding elevated terrain allows them to fire onto the confined unit and then use the surrounding mountains for an escape where pursuit is difficult or impossible (Figure 5-2).

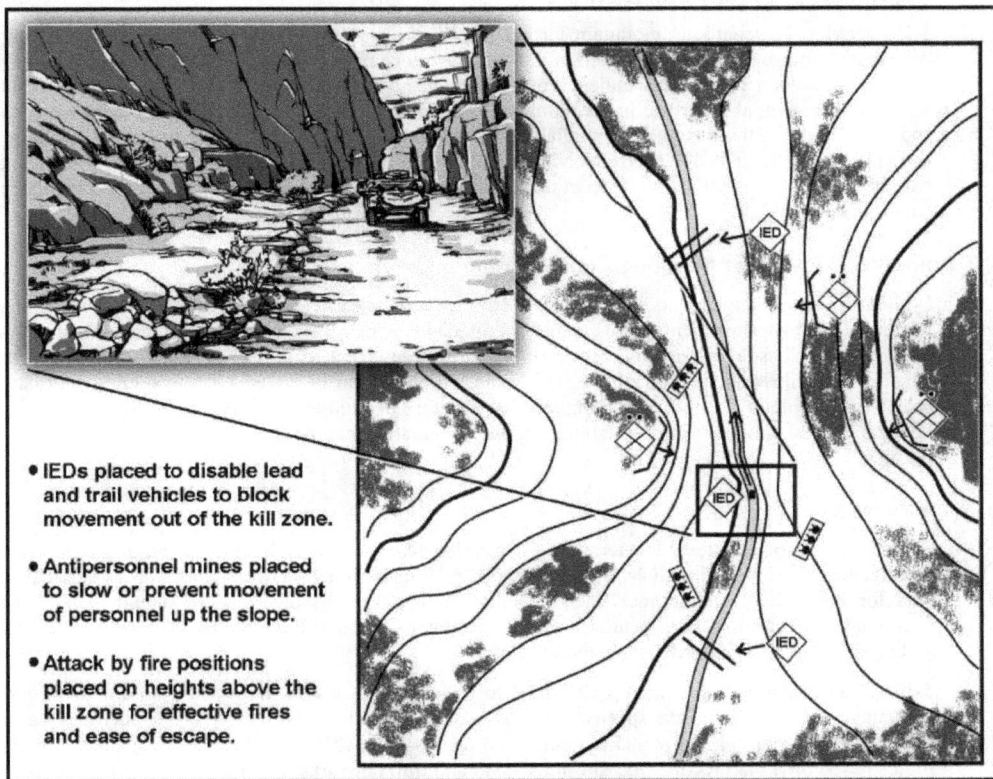

● IEDs placed to disable lead and trail vehicles to block movement out of the kill zone.

● Antipersonnel mines placed to slow or prevent movement of personnel up the slope.

● Attack by fire positions placed on heights above the kill zone for effective fires and ease of escape.

Figure 5-2. Enemy ambush on a narrow mountain pass

5-8.   During movement planning, key points to consider for mounted movements include—
- Establishment of an overwatching element during movement.
- Transportation of units as far as possible by vehicle, until dismounted operations are required to help conserve Soldier strength and energy.
- Dismounted troops interspaced with vehicles to provide security and route clearance.
- Vehicles carrying only drivers, gunners, and supplies while others walk to provide security and overwatch.

- Plans for extended movement times. Dismounted troops may have to bound forward to establish overwatch positions or clear dead space before vehicles can proceed.
- Ground guides for driving in steep or difficult mountain terrain.
- Reduction of tire pressure to increase traction and performance.
- Driver knowledge of techniques for using brake/throttle modulation and use of the transmission to assist in braking in steep and broken terrain.

EFFECTS ON DISMOUNTED MOVEMENT

5-9.   Different types of rock and varying degrees of slope greatly affect dismounted movement and present unique hazards. Dismounted movements should be calculated, deliberate operations. Constantly changing slopes slow foot movements and tire personnel. Distances that normally take an hour or two in flat terrain may take all day to traverse. High altitude effects on personnel further compound energy issues and decrease the efficiency of dismounted movements. Due to the inaccessibility of vehicles, personnel on foot will often be required to carry heavy loads of personal and combat equipment, creating additional stress and further slowing dismounted movements.

5-10. Moving in hazardous mountain terrain, especially during limited visibility conditions, can easily contribute to personnel casualties even in the absence of enemy forces. A 1-meter ledge rapidly traversed in daylight presents a significant challenge or obstacle at night or during other limited visibility conditions. Ambient light available for use in the mountains most often comes from natural sources such as the moon and stars. Usually, there is no light available from manmade sources. Without natural ambient light, depth perception with the naked eye suffers. Night vision goggles can help when some ambient light is available but they too can distort depth perception creating an additional hazard. Rapid movement under these conditions is difficult.

Dismounted Movement Planning Considerations

5-11. Dismounted movements in mountain terrain are tough physically and mentally but are often required for level II and III movements. Movements are often slow, deliberate, and exhausting. Commanders should allow for ample soldier rest and recovery time between tiring, difficult movements through mountain terrain, and follow-on mission objectives. Soldier strength can be saved by transporting units as far as possible by vehicles or other transportation assets before beginning a dismounted portion of an operation. Leaders should monitor Soldier fatigue to ensure carelessness does not result in non-combat related injuries.

Route Selection

5-12. Leaders should study the terrain to determine feasible routes for an operation. A pre-operations intelligence effort should include topographic and photographic map coverage as well as detailed weather data for the area of operations. When planning mountain operations, leaders should gather additional information concerning size, location, and characteristics of landforms, drainage, types of rock and soil, and density and distribution of vegetation.

5-13. When possible, units should add trails to their maps to aid in route selection and rapid mountain movements. Trails often add speed over cross country or direct line movements but increase risk. In addition, maps may not show many washes and depressions which could deceive leaders while selecting routes based on a map recon. Due to limited road and trail networks, and for security purposes, direct line or cross-country navigation may be necessary. Units may consider alternatively traveling on and off trails to gain speed and minimize risk.

5-14. While selecting movement routes, leaders should analyze all contributing factors, including security, feasibility, distance, time, and Soldier fatigue during and after movement. Faster routes may be less secure while more secure routes often take more time. Shorter routes may be more fatiguing than longer ones. Movement control should be decentralized to lower levels as much as possible to allow flexibility along selected routes. Varied terrain, erratic weather, and communication problems inherent to mountain environments may cause changes to the selected route during mission execution.

5-15. Commanders should consider the use of an advance element for selecting and possibly marking routes if necessary. Advance elements may be used to identify hazards such as hidden crevices under snow or ice or to mark dangerous movements along steep grades during limited visibility conditions. The advantages and disadvantages of marking a route should be considered as they may be detected by the enemy, creating conditions for a loss of surprise or an enemy ambush.

5-16. During selection of a dismounted movement routes based on terrain analysis, commanders should include considerations for—
- Enemy situation.
- Time available.
- Skill of troops.
- Equipment available.
- Natural obstacles.
- Weather.
- Compartmentalization of terrain.
- Military crest.

Security During Movements

5-17. Commanders should maintain constant security for their units by selecting proper routes and movement techniques. During movement planning, security related considerations include—
- Overwatch. When moving in the mountains, platoons should use overwatching techniques. Lead platoons secure the high ground and provide overwatching fires as the rest of the company crosses at a lower elevation.
- Silhouetting. If moving along a ridgeline, platoons should avoid silhouetting and move without allowing observation against the skyline. Moving just below the ridgeline avoids silhouetting and completely masks movements from the other side of the ridge.
- Cover and concealment. Companies should use mountain terrain features and vegetation to mask movements. Movement above the timberline reduces the amount of protective cover and concealment available at lower elevations.
- Multiple routes. To reduce vulnerability to the enemy, subordinate units should move separated from each other on multiple and unlikely routes if possible. Special assault climbing teams may be used to construct fixed ropes, hauling systems, traverse systems, and other unique mountaineering systems to provide access to higher elevation levels and alternate movement routes.

Terrain Class Mobility

5-18. Mountain terrain is operationally divided into terrain levels I, II, and III as described in Chapter 1. For movement purposes, the general mobility classifications of unrestricted, restricted, severely restricted terrain is more closely defined for mountain terrain. Mountain terrain is categorized into five classes for mountain movements based on the type of individual movement skill required to traverse it as shown in Table 5-2. Operations conducted in Class 1 and 2 require little to no mountaineering skills. Operations in Classes 3, 4, and 5 require a higher level of mountaineering skills for safe and efficient movement. Commanders should include this type of terrain analysis during planning and preparation for mountain operations.

Table 5-2. Terrain class mobility

Class	Terrain	Mobility Requirements	Skill Level Required	General Mobility and Equipment
1	Gentler slopes/trails.	Walking techniques.	Unskilled.	Easy: Movement generally does not require specialized gear. A simple hand line or fixed rope may aid in movement.
2	Steeper/rugged terrain.	Some use of hands.		
3	Easy climbing.	Fixed ropes where exposed.	Unskilled (with some assistance) and Basic Mountaineers.	Moderate: (exposed 3rd Class) Use of fixed ropes required due to the injury potential of a fall.
4	Steep/exposed climbing.	Fixed ropes required.	Basic Mountaineers (with assistance from assault climbers).	Technical mountaineering equipment will be required to negotiate the terrain. Hard: (exposed 4th class) Requires fixed ropes, high lines, and/or hauling systems.
5	Near vertical.	Technical climbing required.	Assault climbers.	All members of the patrol should be proficient at moving on these systems as a fall may be catastrophic.

Effects of Slope on Dismounted Movement

5-19. The rise and fall of the ground is known as the slope or gradient (grade). Slopes of 7 percent or greater affect the movement speed along a route and are considered an obstruction. The percent of slope is used to describe the effect that inclines have on movement rates. It is the ratio of the change in elevation (the vertical distance to the horizontal ground distance) multiplied by 100. When planning routes, leaders should factor elevation gain and loss, as much as distance, into their movement timelines as the effects of slope on dismounted movement is significant. (For a complete description of slope calculation, see FM 3-34.170.)

5-20. As the percentage of slope increases, movement rates decrease due to the increase in energy and physical demands needed for movement. Moving to the same location using an indirect route can help reduce the amount of strenuous energy needed but increases time needed due to the total amount of terrain traversed. Regardless of whether the unit is moving uphill or downhill, movement rates are decreased.

5-21. Slopes covered in talus often prove to be a relatively easy ascent route. On the other hand, climbing a scree slope can be extremely difficult, as the small rocks tend to loosen easily and give way. This characteristic often makes scree fields excellent descent routes. Before attempting to descend scree slopes, commanders should carefully analyze the potential for creating dangerous rockfall and take necessary avoidance measures.

Dismounted Movement Rates

5-22. A Soldier can only move as fast as his lungs and legs will allow. A trained, conditioned, and acclimatized Soldier often has endurance and moves efficiently. Rest, good nutrition and hydration, conditioning, acclimatization, proper training, and the will to climb are key. Terrain, weather, and light conditions also affect movement rates. Movement rates should be relative to the conditions. The more adverse the conditions, the slower the pace should be. Moving too fast, even under ideal conditions, can produce early fatigue, require more rest halts, and result in time loss. Dismounted movement rates for mountain environments are shown in Table 5-3 below.

Table 5-3. Dismounted movement rates

Movement Mode	Unbroken Trail	Broken Trail
On foot, no snow cover.	2 to 3 kph – cross country.	3 to 4 kph – trail walking.
On foot, no ski or snowshoe. Less than 1 foot of snow.	1.5 to 3 kph.	2 to 3 kph.
On foot, no ski or snowshoe. More than 1 foot of snow.	.5 to 1 kph.	2 to 3 kph.
Snowshoe.	1.5 to 3 kph.	3 to 4 kph.
Skiing.	1.5 to 5 kph.	5 to 6 kph.
Skijoring.	NA	8 to 24 kph (for safety, 15 kph is the highest recommended speed).

Abbreviations
kph   kilometers per hour.
NA   not applicable.

Note: Add 1 hour for every 300 meters of ascent and 1 hour for every 600 meters of descent.

5-23. Movement rates, coupled with proper Soldier spacing, should be adjusted to prevent an accordion effect during movement in mountain terrain. The spacing between Soldiers largely depends on the mission, the terrain, and visibility. Soldiers should allow enough distance between themselves to climb without causing the following individual to change pace. In mountain terrain, a slow, steady pace is preferred to more rapid movement with frequent halts.

5-24. To help minimize Soldier fatigue and ensure efficiency, the following should be considered during movement rate evaluation:

- When traveling at a moderate pace, the need for rest halts can decrease and the chance of personnel overheating will often be less than traveling at a high a rate. Minimization of halts enables units to cover a given distance in minimal time.

- An adjustment halt should be taken during the first half-hour of movement. Soldiers can loosen or tighten bootlaces as needed, adjust packs, and add or remove layers of clothing as appropriate.

- Short rest halts may be taken every 1 to 1.5 hours. If possible, Soldiers should lean against a tree, rock, or hillside to relieve their shoulders of pack weight, breathe deeply, hydrate, and snack on trail food. Halts should be short (1 to 2 minutes) to avoid muscles stiffening. Take rests on level ground, if possible, and avoid steep inclines.

- Longer rest halts may be taken later in the march if necessary due to fatigue or mission requirements. At these halts, Soldiers may need to put on additional clothing to avoid becoming chilled. It is much easier to keep a warm body warm than to warm up a cold one.

- After a climb, Soldiers need a good rest to revive tired muscles. Use a rest stop for steep slopes, snowfields, and higher elevations. Rest stops help control the pace and limits fatigue by giving the lungs and legs a moment to recuperate between stops. Maintain a slow and rhythmic pace.

- Soldiers should employ proper walking techniques and pause briefly after each step forward, relaxing the muscles of the forward leg while resting his entire body weight on the rear leg. The rear leg should be kept straight with the knee locked so that bone, not muscle, supports the weight. After relaxing the forward leg, Soldiers should scan their surroundings and ensure they focus on maintaining alertness and not just traversing the terrain.

- Soldiers should synchronize their breathing with each rest step. The number of breaths per step changes depending upon the difficulty of the climb. Steeper slopes or higher elevations may require several breaths per step. It is especially important to breathe deeply when the air thins at higher altitude, using the "pressure breathing" technique. The Soldier should exhale strongly, enabling an easier, deeper inhale. This slow, steady, halting rest step is more efficient than spurts of speed, which is rapidly exhausting and requires longer recovery.

Movements During Adverse Weather

5-25. Terrain and weather often restrict planned movements. Commanders should be prepared for wide variations in temperature and the various types and amounts of precipitation often experienced in mountain environments by erratic weather conditions. Storms reduce visibility during movements and severe storms may dictate halting movements and seeking shelter. When the tactical situation requires continued movement during a storm, leaders should attempt to avoid:

- Using ravines as movement routes due to flash floods.
- High pinnacles and ridgelines during electrical storms.
- Areas of potential avalanche or rock-fall.

Vertical Danger Areas

5-26. In mountain environments, units will eventually have to cross steep terrain that requires additional equipment and climbing skills. These areas are often labeled as vertical danger areas. These crossings may require fixed ropes, rappels, or a suspension traverse. Soldiers trained on these systems and the techniques for their employment are required to ensure safety during movement. The same principles that apply to crossing linear danger areas, as described in FM 3-21.8, apply to vertical danger areas including near and far side security. Units should have trained personnel at key points to ensure less trained personnel move safely along any fixed ropes. Actions on contact procedures should be established and rehearsed for contact experienced while moving along a fixed rope system.

Movement Over Snow

5-27. Snow and ice makes traction less stable, increasing the risk of injury from slips and falls. A slip near a steep mountain slope can quickly turn fatal if proper precautions are not taken. In addition to causing challenges for traction, snow is particularly dangerous due to hidden underlying hazards including cracks, crevices, and deep ravines. Movement over snow may require the aid of additional equipment such as snow shoes or other equipment. Specialized personnel or techniques may also be required depending on the terrain, slope, and depth of the snow. (For an in depth discussion of movement over snow and ice, see FM 3-97.61.)

Individual Movement Techniques

5-28. The basic principles of mountain walking remain the same whether it is up scree or talus, through boulder fields or steep wooded mountainsides, or over snow or grass-covered slopes. Soldiers should keep their weight centered directly over their feet at all times. Feet should be placed on the ground in order to obtain as much (boot) sole–ground contact as possible. Footing should be on the uphill side of grass tussocks, small talus, and other level spots to avoid twisting an ankle or straining an Achilles tendon. Straighten the knee after each step and allow for rest between steps. Take moderate steps at a steady pace. Avoid any angle of ascent or descent that is too steep, and use indentations in the slope to the advantage.

5-29. In addition to proper technique, pace should be adapted to conditions. Soldiers should set a tempo, or number of steps per minute, according to the pace of the unit in which he is moving. Individuals should maintain their tempo while compensating for changes in slope or terrain by adjusting the length of their stride. Tempo, pace, and rhythm are enhanced when an interval of three to five paces is kept between individuals. This interval helps lessen the accordion effect of people at the end of the file who must constantly stop and start.

5-30. Downhill walking uses less energy than uphill walking but is much harder on the body. Stepping down can hammer the full body weight onto the feet and legs. Blisters, blackened toenails, knee damage, and back pain may follow. To avoid these problems, Soldiers should start by tightening bootlaces to ensure a snug fit and keep toenails trimmed. Keep a moderate pace and walk with knees flexed to absorb shock.

5-31. Soldiers should be extremely cautious while traveling on the side of a hill. During side-hill travel personnel are more vulnerable to twisted ankles, back injury, and loss of balance when weighted down with a rucksack. During side-hill travel, attempt to switchback periodically if possible and use any lower-angle flat areas, such as rocks, animal trails, and the ground above grass or brush clumps, to level off the route.

Specialized Equipment and Skills

5-32. Depending upon the particular operation and the terrain itself, companies may find that they eventually have to cross terrain that requires a higher level of training and specialized equipment. Movement across this type of terrain often involves the use of ropes, mountaineering kits, and assault climbers.

Ropes

5-33. The most common type of rope installation in the mountains is the fixed rope system. A fixed rope is a rope anchored in place to assist Soldiers in movement over difficult terrain. Its simplest form is a rope tied off at the top of steep terrain. As terrain becomes steeper or more difficult, fixed rope systems may require intermediate anchors along the route. Moving on a fixed rope requires minimal equipment. The use of harnesses, ascenders, and other technical gear makes fixed rope movement easier, faster, and safer, but adds to total mission weight (Figure 5-3).

Figure 5-3. Using a fixed rope system

5-34. Squad slings and short ropes are valuable when the terrain becomes difficult. Body belays may be necessary at times and should be rehearsed by all company personnel prior to operations. (For extensive detail on the use of ropes, rope systems, and the care maintenance of ropes see FM 3-97.61.)

Mountaineering Kits

5-35. The Army mountaineering kits are made up of three separate but integrated kits of state of the art, commercial equipment which meet the highest industry standards. The separate kits enable the commander to tailor the equipment to the mission environment.

High Angle Mountaineering Kit

5-36. The High Angle Mountaineering Kit (HAMK) is designed for a minimally-trained Infantry Brigade Combat Team Platoon (40 personnel) moving through steep terrain, void of ice or snow, on rope installations established by assault climbers. The HAMK provides each Soldier in the platoon with a harness, locking and nonlocking carabineers, sewn webbing runners, 7-mm accessory cord, and a belay/rappel device. There are also static installation ropes, a rope cutter and a rope washer (Figure 5-4).

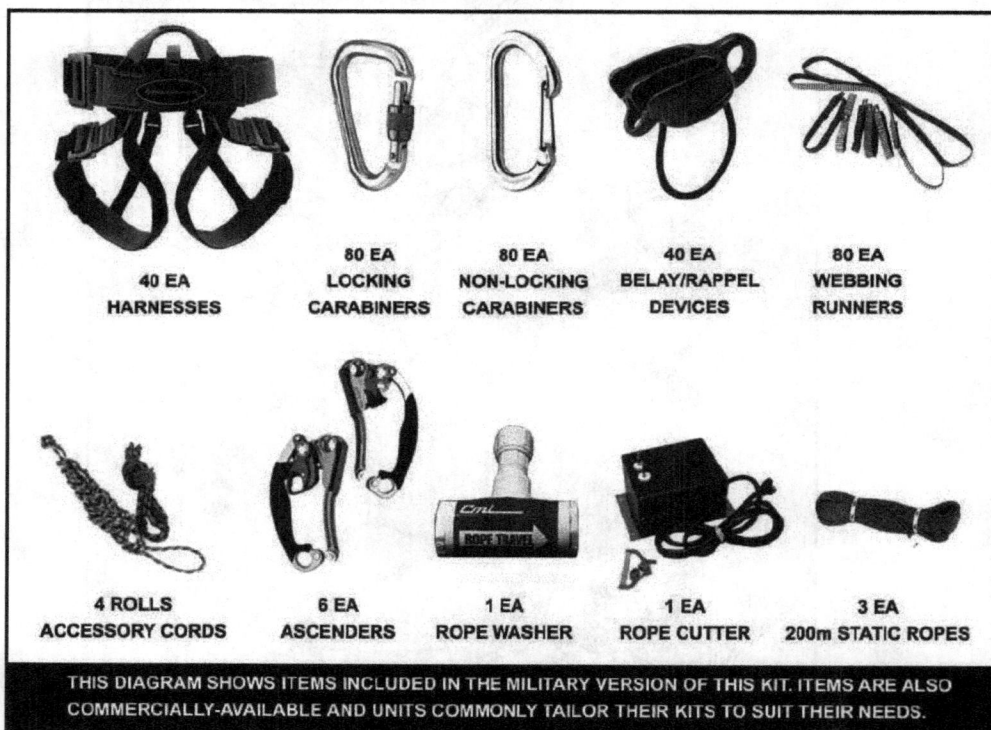

| 40 EA HARNESSES | 80 EA LOCKING CARABINERS | 80 EA NON-LOCKING CARABINERS | 40 EA BELAY/RAPPEL DEVICES | 80 EA WEBBING RUNNERS |

| 4 ROLLS ACCESSORY CORDS | 6 EA ASCENDERS | 1 EA ROPE WASHER | 1 EA ROPE CUTTER | 3 EA 200m STATIC ROPES |

THIS DIAGRAM SHOWS ITEMS INCLUDED IN THE MILITARY VERSION OF THIS KIT. ITEMS ARE ALSO COMMERCIALLY-AVAILABLE AND UNITS COMMONLY TAILOR THEIR KITS TO SUIT THEIR NEEDS.

Figure 5-4. HAMK

Assault Climber Team Kit

5-37. The Assault Climber Team Kit (ACTK) is used by a trained assault climber team of three personnel to establish rope installations that minimally-trained Soldiers can move over using the HAMK. The ACTK provides each Soldier in the assault climber team with a harness, locking and non-locking carabineers, sewn webbing runners, mechanical ascenders, chock pick, assault climber bag, 7-mm accessory cord, and a belay/rappel device. There are also dynamic climbing ropes and rock protection equipment including spring loaded camming devices and chocks (Figure 5-5).

Figure 5-5. ACTK

Snow and Ice Mobility Kit

5-38. The Snow and Ice Mobility Kit (SIMK) is used by an Infantry platoon trained in the techniques of operating in steep terrain covered by snow or ice. The SIMK provides each Soldier in the platoon an avalanche transceiver, crampons, ice axe, and snowshoes. There are also avalanche shovels, probes and ice and snow anchors included (Figure 5-6).

Assault Climbers

5-39. Assault climbers are responsible for the rigging, inspection, use, and operation of all basic rope systems. They are trained in additional rope management skills, knot tying, and belay and rappel techniques, as well as using specialized mountaineering equipment. Assault climbers are capable of rigging complex, multipoint anchors, and high-angle raising/lowering systems. Units should employ basic mountaineers whenever possible when operating on moderate class 2-4 terrain, and assault climber teams whenever operating on hard class 4 or 5 terrain. Leaders may consider having their reconnaissance and surveillance personnel, including Soldiers assigned to reconnaissance platoons and snipers, as qualified assault climbers. (For additional information on knowledge and skills of assault climbers see FM 3-97.61.)

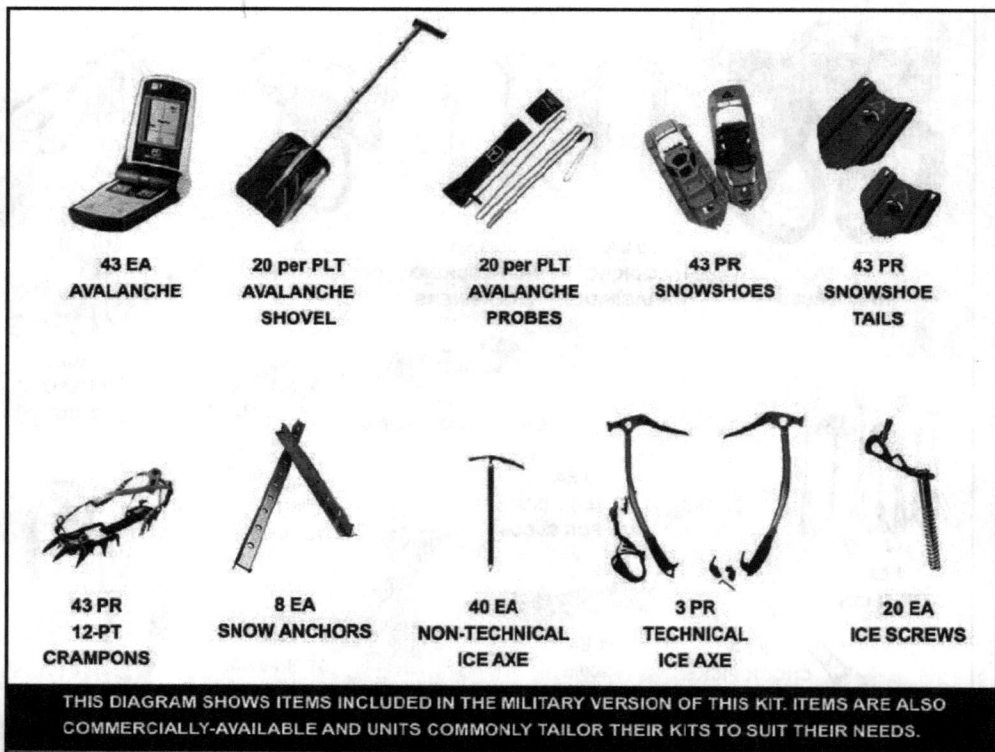

THIS DIAGRAM SHOWS ITEMS INCLUDED IN THE MILITARY VERSION OF THIS KIT. ITEMS ARE ALSO COMMERCIALLY-AVAILABLE AND UNITS COMMONLY TAILOR THEIR KITS TO SUIT THEIR NEEDS.

Figure 5-6. SIMK

EFFECTS ON AIR MOVEMENT

5-40. Movement of personnel and supplies by air can be relatively quick and efficient and is widely used in mountain operations. While air movement conserves time and energy, limited aircraft, mountain terrain, and weather conditions can place restrictions on air movement.

Air Movement Planning Considerations

5-41. Flying can be an extremely dangerous operation in mountain terrain and is aggravated further when coupled with potential enemy contact. The use of aircraft in mountain environments should be a carefully planned and executed operation. U.S. forces rely heavily on helicopters for transportation and movement in the mountains, requiring aviation planners to be involved in the planning process early. Commanders should become intimately familiar with the conditions that may limit the full effectiveness of Army aviation when considering their use for an operation in a mountain environment. Determining when aircraft may or may not fly, where they may fly, and what weight limitations they have for a particular mission results from a combination of factors that largely include terrain and weather conditions. Commanders can obtain that type data from the brigade aviation element to use during the planning of operations that include air assets. (For more information see FM 3-04.203.)

Weather

5-42. Weather can cancel the use of aircraft for extended periods in mountain climates. Sudden weather changes may also preclude the use of aircraft scheduled for company movements for a particular mission. Leaders should consider whether those same restrictions preclude the use of aircraft if needed for casualty evacuation.

5-43. Utility and cargo helicopters remain key to the rapid movement of Soldiers and equipment in the mountains. Even so, any operation that depends primarily on continuous aviation support to succeed is extremely risky. High elevations and rapidly changing and severe weather common to mountain environments restrict aviation operations and can make availability of aviation support unpredictable. At high altitudes, weather that appears to be stable to the ground observer may significantly affect helicopters. During the planning of operations, leaders should account for contingencies based on changing weather conditions that may affect aircraft.

Altitude

5-44. High altitude atmospheric changes can have a dramatic effect on air platforms. As elevation increases, air density decreases, air becomes thinner, icing is common, and lift is decreased. At some point lift decreases to the extent that aircraft can no longer remain airborne. Certain mountain ranges and peaks are simply too high for some rotary-winged aircraft to cross.

5-45. Even though the terrain, weather, and mission variables allow for movement by air, commanders should also consider the effect of altitude on Soldiers when planning movement of personnel. If possible, commanders should use Soldiers acclimatized at or above the elevation level planned for the air movement. Depending on the situation, it may be better to have troops walk in rather than fly into the necessary elevation level allowing them more time for acclimatization.

Landing Zones

5-46. In planning the use of aircraft, suitable LZs must also be designated. Terrain suitable for multiple helicopter LZs in mountain environments may be limited. A level area suitable for a mountain LZ is usually firm enough to support helicopters and frequently requires little preparation beyond the clearance of loose material. If possible, LZs should be located where aircraft can take off and land into the wind and without restrictions from surrounding terrain. Helicopters should attempt to land on relatively level terrain whenever possible. Slope landing is possible but should be coordinated with the aircraft due to variations in aircraft restrictions. Aircraft should avoid landing on a down slope (Figure 5-7).

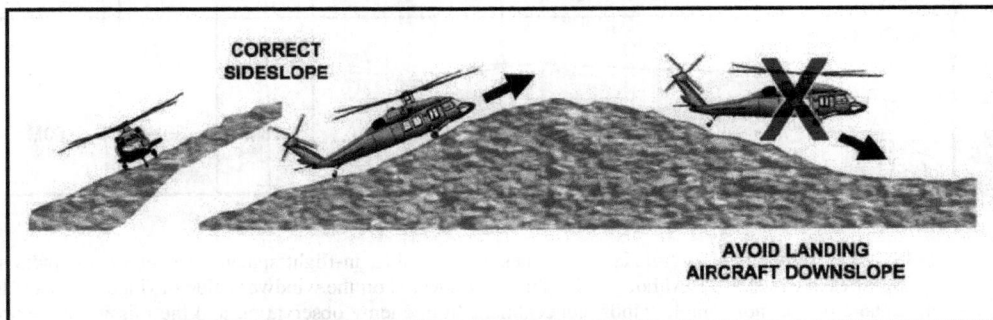

CORRECT SIDESLOPE

AVOID LANDING AIRCRAFT DOWNSLOPE

Figure 5-7. Helicopter slope landings

5-47. If LZs must be constructed, clearing may be difficult due to the rocky ground. Stand-off space from rock wall faces should be cleared and a level landing surface created. Demolitions may be required to clear large rocks but care should be used to prevent rockslides or avalanches started by the explosive shock. During the winter, snow should be packed to prevent whiteouts. Similarly, sandy or dusty LZs should be dampened with water to prevent brownouts. Minimum requirements for helicopter landing zones are shown in Table 5-4.

Table 5-4. Helicopter landing zone requirements

HARD SURFACE:
Vegetation cut to 1 foot (.3M)
(will support aircraft)

OBSTRUCTION FREE:
Vegetation cut to 2 feet (.6M)

SURFACE CLEARED:
Vegetation cut to 1 foot (.3M)

LANDING POINT	MINIMUM DIAMETER OF LANDING POINT	HARD SURFACE	SURFACE CLEARED	OBSTRUCTION FREE
SIZE 1 - Light Observation OH-58D OH-6	25M	5M	15M	25M
SIZE 2 - Light Utility and Attack UH-1H H-65 AH-1W	35M	10M	20M	35M
SIZE 3 - Medium Utility and Attack UH-60 H-2 AH-64	50M	15M	35M	50M
SIZE 4 - Cargo CH-47 CH-53	80M	15M	35M	80M

5-48. When only single aircraft landing zones are available, in-flight spacing between helicopters should be significantly increased. Although LZs should be located on the windward side of ridges or peaks to take advantage of the more stable winds, concealment from enemy observation and the mission are extremely important factors in site selection in forward areas.

5-49. Rotary-wing aircraft may be forced to insert personnel from a low hover, by rappelling, or by fastrope if an LZ is not available. Equipment and supplies may have to be delivered or dropped without landing as well. When it is impossible for helicopters to land, personnel may rappel and light equipment may be sling-loaded, dropped, or lowered by rope at an insertion point while the helicopter hovers. This may increase turnaround time and aircraft vulnerability. Since available landing sites are often limited, the enemy can be expected to target all likely locations. Personnel should secure terrain that dominates an LZ to increase security and coordinate for suppression of enemy air defense weapons during air assault operations.

5-50. The terrain, weather, and potential for enemy actions make landings a risky aspect of air movements. Units should assume LZs are being observed by the enemy and plan accordingly.

Flight Routes

5-51. Rugged, mountain terrain complicates flight route selection and places an additional navigational load and strain on the entire crew. There is little margin for error for aircraft flying near the mountains. Direct routes can seldom be flown without exposing aircraft to an unacceptable risk of detection and targeting by the enemy. Tactical flight routes follow valley corridors, where it is possible to obtain cover and concealment while maintaining the highest possible terrain flight altitude. Terrain flight routes in the mountains may preclude using closed formations. Multi-helicopter operations are normally flown in "loose" or "staggered trail" formations with increased spacing between aircraft.

Loads

5-52. During passenger moves, passengers and equipment for multiple destinations may be carried. Aircrews plan accordingly to ensure minimal time is spent in off-load and on-load procedures, but delays on the LZ can occur. This increases the risk of detection by enemy personnel and increases the risk of damage or destruction from enemy direct or indirect fires.

5-53. As altitude increases and lift and aircraft power available decreases, the ability for aircraft to carry a full combat load decreases. For high altitude operations during air assaults or air movements, this may result in fewer Soldiers and less equipment per aircraft. This may require units to plan for more aircraft or more chalks during missions. Coordination with aircrews during the mission planning process enable the commander to plan adequately for such contingencies.

OTHER MOVEMENT ASSETS

5-54. The use of non-standard means of transportation to aid in movements is routine in mountain environments. This is especially true in third world countries where forces often operate. The use of pack animals, for example, to aid in the movement of supplies and equipment is a standard practice in many mountain environments. (See Chapter 6 of this manual for more information.)

5-55. Other mobility assets that can aid in movement of personnel, equipment, and supplies include terrain vehicles, nonstandard tactical vehicles, and motorcycles. Many of these assets can be purchased or contracted from the host nation. While military vehicles tend to be more robust, often these vehicles are better designed to maneuver or travel on available mountain roads and trails.

PATROLS

5-56. Mountain environments often span vast distances with friendly units operating in noncontiguous AOs. Some locations, such as certain key terrain, villages, strongpoints, and other areas, may be strongly defended. Often there are other large areas where neither friendly nor enemy units are concerned with the retention of terrain. Enemy operating in these areas is often more concerned with inflicting damage on friendly forces than on holding or defending a piece of ground. In this type of environment the enemy often engages friendly units at the time and place of their choosing and then leaves the area. This makes planning offensive operations a challenge and often does not create many opportunities for planned deliberate attacks. For this reason, mountain operations conducted by Infantry units are often conducted using combat patrols.

5-57. In the offense, combat patrols may be in the form of a raid or an ambush. Raid and ambush combat patrols are normally conducted against known or suspected locations where the enemy is or is expected to be. (For more information on raids and ambushes in the mountains see Chapter 3 of this manual.) In mountain combat operations, reconnaissance and security patrols have been used extensively. Each patrol mission should have a clear task and purpose. Commanders and leaders should clearly understand the objective and actions taken upon enemy contact for each patrol.

5-58. Regardless of the type of patrol, techniques for movement through the mountains while on patrol are similar. In the mountains, moving elements of the patrol should be covered by another overwatching element of the patrol (Figure 5-8). The bounding of sub elements to overwatch the movements of other elements is vital to maintaining security. Leaders should assume they are being observed by the enemy throughout their entire mission. Patrols should also be conducted within range and cover of indirect fires, air assets, or both. Operations without these covering fires expose the patrol to extreme risks. If the availability of aircraft is limited, the need for available indirect fire coverage increases.

Figure 5-8. Overwatching a patrol

5-59. A unique characteristic of fighting in the mountains, especially against an enemy familiar with the terrain is that the enemy is hard to find. Mountain terrain can offer protection from observation to those not wanting to be seen or discovered. Contact is often initiated by the enemy rather than by friendly units. When contact is made, it is often in the form of an ambush with standoff and egress routes for the enemy.

5-60. Reconnaissance and security patrols are conducted in the mountains for varied purposes. Reconnaissance patrols are also used to help determine, prepare for, or enhance follow-on offensive operations. They are sent out to detect or observe enemy actions, and to look for signs of enemy forces or actions such as enemy caches, trails, caves, tunnels, or other signs of enemy presence. Reconnaissance patrols do not seek to make physical contact with the enemy but are used to gain information.

5-61. In contrast to reconnaissance patrols, security patrols are often attempts to make contact with the enemy or are associated with protection of an area, such as a unit location or key terrain. These patrols are often sent out to patrol areas with poor observation or fields of fire. They seek to make enemy contact but should be covered by indirect or air assets. Security patrols are often used as an integral part of defensive operations in mountain environments. Commanders use security patrols to cover unobservable areas and keep the enemy out of the area. During the conduct of security patrols, Soldiers become familiar with their surroundings—making it easier to spot something that may indicate a potential enemy action.

Patrol base

5-62. When a unit halts for an extended period while patrolling, they often establish a patrol base. In mountain operations, patrol bases are often used due to the remote, difficult terrain in which patrolling operations are conducted. Patrols may often be conducted for extended periods requiring the establishment of one or more patrol bases. While occupying a patrol base, both active and passive measures should be taken to provide maximum protection. The leader selects an area that provides passive security from enemy detection and organizes the base and his personnel for occupation. Common situations that require establishment of a patrol base include—

- A requirement to cease all movement to avoid detection.
- A requirement to hide the unit during a lengthy, detailed reconnaissance of the objective area.

- A need to prepare food, maintain weapons and equipment, and rest after extended movement.
- A need to formulate a final plan and issue orders for actions at the objective.
- A requirement for reorganization after a patrol has infiltrated the enemy area in small groups (used in conjunction with a linkup point).
- A need for a base from where several consecutive or concurrent operations such as ambush, raid, reconnaissance, or surveillance patrols can be conducted.

5-63. Evacuation of a patrol base depends on the degree of control the enemy force has in the base area, their ability to react to the discovery of a base, and their ability to affect the unit's mission. When an enemy force is relatively small and weak, patrol base secrecy may not be an overriding consideration and evacuation may or may not be necessary. In an area controlled by a larger enemy force or where safety of unit personnel is compromised, evacuation may be required.

5-64. Patrol bases established in mountain terrain offer unique challenges. Units establishing patrol bases should quickly learn how to use the terrain to their advantage. They should equally ensure they do not offer the enemy a chance to capitalize on opportunities created by the establishment of a patrol base in a poor location. Leaders should avoid establishment of a patrol base during daylight hours if possible. Patrols may stage during daylight but should move to a new location during darkness. Moving at night can confuse the enemy and keep him guessing as to the patrols location. If possible, leaders should also attempt to overwatch a previously occupied patrol base for enemy activity.

5-65. During establishment of a patrol base in mountain terrain, an important consideration is a terrain analysis. Ravines, depressions, irrigation tunnels, ditches, and other features offer unobservable avenues of approach for enemy personnel. While not always possible to completely avoid areas without these features, base selection should include how these areas will be covered for security of the base. Observation posts require manpower but may be established to increase security of the base and cover some avenues of approach. Leaders should consider covering some avenues effectively by using early warning signaling devices and claymore mines.

Mounted Patrols

5-66. The upper levels of mountain terrain are generally not well suited for mounted patrols. While some mounted patrolling can be accomplished, patrolling often involves a combination of both mounted and dismounted movement. Dismounted movement through mountain terrain can be exhausting. To help maintain Soldier strength and energy, units often use some sort of vehicle transportation to move up to or closer to the actual targeted patrol area. Usually this is to a point where the vehicles can no longer effectively travel or to a point that best accommodates the intended mission. At that point, the unit dismounts and continues with the mission.

5-67. Dismounted Infantry units may be augmented with military vehicles, allowing them to conduct mounted patrolling. They may also procure some other type vehicles. Use gators or four-wheel drive all-terrain vehicles to conduct mounted patrolling and can travel into areas non-negotiable by military vehicles.

5-68. Mountain terrain offers many opportunities for enemy ambushes or other hostile actions, especially along known restrictive roads, routes, or paths where vehicles must travel. The terrain generally affects a leader's decision on vehicle spacing and speed, and often dictates a column style formation due to the restrictiveness of the routes. As with all patrols, mounted patrols should be within the covering fires of artillery or aviation assets. Patrolling outside these conditions is extremely risky.

5-69. In planning mounted patrols, leaders should determine a specific task and purpose for the patrol and consider all mission variables along with particular considerations for—

- Procedures for enemy contact.
- Mounted and dismounted portions of the patrol.
- Location of vehicles during dismounted operations.
- Carrying mortars with the patrol for indirect support.
- Use of artillery and air assets.
- Recovery options for damaged or disabled vehicles.

- CASEVAC/MEDEVAC procedures.
- Length of patrol.

Dismounted Patrols

5-70. Dismounted patrolling in mountain terrain encompasses all the fundamentals of patrolling in other environments with special considerations on the unique aspects the mountains create. Generally, all tasks involved in dismounted operations slow down as altitude increases. Dismounted patrolling in mountain terrain is tedious, exhausting, and physically and mentally demanding. Thin air at high altitude, rugged terrain, and extreme weather conditions create an environment that can quickly drain the strength and endurance of Soldiers. Slower operations at high altitudes often result in less terrain coverage during each patrol. Soldiers should remain vigilant while on patrol and avoid the tendency to concentrate on moving, climbing, and traversing obstacles rather than staying alert to their surroundings.

5-71. One important factor commanders should consider while planning dismounted patrols in mountain terrain is use of an overwatching element. A typical mountain patrol often consists of one or two squads. One element, a squad or a fire team, overwatches the other as they move. Position the overwatching element on terrain, most often high ground, where they can effectively cover the movements of the moving element. They should pay particular attention to areas such as depressions, cracks, crevices, rock formations, and draws where enemy personnel can easily hide undetected by the moving unit.

5-72. Dismounted patrolling in mountain environments often begins with movement by some means of transportation to or near the area to be patrolled. If vehicles are used to transport personnel to a dismount location, leaders have two main options when considering what to do with the vehicles after drop off. The first option is to send the vehicles to another more secure staging area or back to the area they departed from, such as a combat outpost or other base, until needed for pick up of personnel. The second option is to leave the vehicles in or near the drop off location where they can emplace the heavier 120-mm mortar in support of the patrol. The decision on what to do with the vehicles relies on many factors with some of the main considerations being—

- Use of available covering artillery or mortar fires.
- Security of the vehicles and personnel remaining with the vehicles.
- CASEVAC/MEDEVAC procedures.
- Length of the patrol.

5-73. Leaders should also determine what their Soldiers carry with them on a dismounted patrol. Leaders should ensure Soldiers only carry what is necessary for the duration of the mission. Body armor, weapons, and ammunition all weigh the Soldier down. Assault packs often consist of little more than water, food, additional ammunition, a lightweight blanket, survival gear, and some medical supplies. If resupply is needed for the patrol, it often comes by way of air since travel back to a resupply pick up location is often much more exhausting and time consuming.

OBSERVATION POSTS

5-74. OPs can vary from a small, two-man occupied position supporting a larger unit, to a platoon-sized position. The primary mission of an OP is to watch and listen for activity, to provide security, and to report identified activity. OPs can be used in the defense of an established company position or positioned to observe and gain information for subsequent offensive actions.

5-75. In mountain terrain the detection of enemy locations can be extremely difficult. An effective way to find the enemy is to see personnel moving in and out of their locations when they believe they are not being watched. OPs used for these purposes tend to be clandestine operations and information gained from them often supports other offensive actions. Observers infiltrate to the OP location and observe without being detected. OP personnel report enemy locations, strengths, and activities in preparation for, during, and after subsequent offensive operations.

5-76. Personnel designated to occupy an OP must be prepared to traverse difficult infiltration routes, especially if the infiltration is to be unobserved. OPs are often placed in high terrain with little or no easy access. Additionally, clandestine operations requiring unobserved infiltration often require movement through unlikely avenues including steep cliffs with a difficult climb. Commanders should consider whether the use of special teams or equipment may be needed to assist in the infiltration and exfiltration of OP personnel.

5-77. Enemy personnel have the same basic needs for sustainment supplies as friendly units and at times must leave their cave, tunnel, or hiding place in order to obtain them. Observers placed in areas or trails known to be used by enemy forces can watch for activity and if needed, adjust their OP position to eventually trace the enemy back to his starting position. Snipers and scouts are ideal for this type of operation as they are both skilled in advanced camouflage and observation techniques.

5-78. Leaders should consider providing OP personnel with available equipment, such as enhanced optics, that could improve their observation activities. Leaders should consider the length of time OP personnel can operate until they need to be relieved.

Site Selection

5-79. Along with all METT-TC considerations, site selection for an OP mainly depends on the mission or purpose for establishing the OP. OPs are often established to overwatch areas where enemy activity is expected, view dead space unobservable from other locations, or to cover likely avenues of approach. Unlike sites selected for covert offensive OPs, defensive OPs are not always established to be unobservable by the enemy. Many OPs are deliberately placed in a particular location to deter enemy activity. These sites may be along supply or movement routes or in a strategic location outside base location. In the mountains, Soldiers may occupy OPs on a mountain ridge overlooking enemy territory in order to assist in denying free access or passage along movement routes (Figure 5-9).

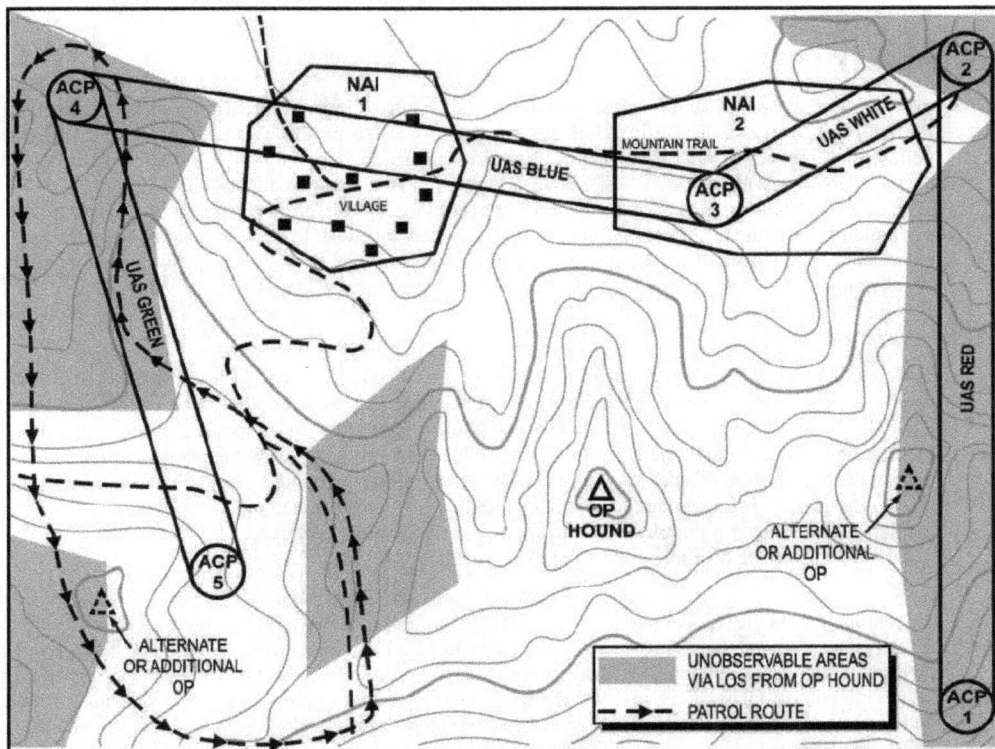

Figure 5-9. Observation post

Enhanced Optics

5-80. Whenever possible, OPs should include enhanced optics systems to aid in observation. These systems are critical for improving operations during limited visibility conditions and greatly aid in long range detail enhancements. Along with company level assets such as the command launch unit, common battalion level and above systems that may be available to a company include the ITAS from a weapons company and the LRAS3 from a reconnaissance troop. These systems can be placed in OPs to aid in long range target surveillance and acquisition.

Improved Target Acquisition System

5-81. The M41 ITAS that accompanies the tube-launched, optically-tracked, wire-guided missile systems is an integrated day/night sight that may be used to enhance observation ability during daylight or limited visibility conditions. This proves to be a tremendous asset for establishing observation posts. The weapons systems provide for defensive measures and in the case of overt OPs, help establish a sense of deterrence for aggressive behavior. Weapons may be either vehicular or ground mounted.

Long Range Advanced Scout Surveillance System

5-82. The LRAS3 is a long-range multi-sensor system that provides real-time detection, recognition, identification and pinpointing of distant target locations. The LRAS3 is deployed on the M1114 high mobility multi-purpose wheeled vehicle in its mounted configuration and can be used on a tripod for dismounted missions. This system provides precise target location by incorporation of advanced second generation forward looking infrared, a global positioning interferometer, an eye-safe laser range finder, and a TV camera.

COMBAT OUTPOSTS

5-83. Mountain operations conducted over large areas have shown a need for establishing multiple small friendly unit locations. These locations enable U.S. forces to protect or maintain contact with the local populace, protect friendly units, control specific areas, and support subordinate unit operations and personnel over a widespread battlefield. In mountain environments, combat outposts have been routinely used for these purposes and are constructed according to the mission, terrain, and relation to other surrounding structures. Defensive plans are established to allow leaders or commanders to operate for extended periods from these defendable positions. The bases are often company sized or smaller and usually supported by a larger battalion size forward operating base. Defensive plans provide security for the personnel within the confines of the position itself, as well as other personnel or areas specifically assigned in their mission.

5-84. Combat outposts should be planned, constructed, and organized to accommodate their particular mission. They range in size, composition, and location depending upon their mission. Commanders often have the freedom to design the dimensions of the outpost to be in concert with the uniqueness of the surrounding terrain and still support the mission. Often a significant difference between individual combat outposts is the relation of each to a populated town or village. Combat outposts located near a population often require less infrastructure development than those in more remote locations. Security may be a greater challenge near a population. Conversely, remote location combat outposts have more flexibility of placement and can be positioned for optimal observation and standoff.

5-85. Defense of a combat outpost in the mountains should concentrate on site design and operating procedures favorable to defending units. Design and operations should concentrate on retaining the initiative by making the enemy react and unable to execute his own offensive plan. Defensive security measures include establishing security plans and positions, clearing, identifying, and controlling dead space, placing obstacles in avenues of approach, creating target reference points and final protective fires, and requesting indirect fire targets. Frequent active patrolling outside the confines of the combat outpost helps guard against covert enemy activity.

SITE SELECTION

5-86. In mountain terrain, the enemy often enjoys freedom of maneuver. This is largely because control of large areas of mountain terrain is extremely difficult and brings with it a unique set of challenges. In Afghanistan, for example, enemy forces use mountain passes to move freely across the Pakistan-Afghanistan border. They use these areas to evade and escape friendly forces and to support their own operations. To counter these actions, establish combat outposts on key terrain to allow control over these areas (Figure 5-10).

5-87. Locations for a combat outpost in mountain environments are often, but not always, associated with the high ground. Combat outposts may also be positioned where they can influence the civilian population such as near villages and road networks. High ground locations can offer all around visibility and standoff from enemy actions. An appropriate location in the right area, of the right size, clear of debris rocks, trees, and other vegetation, may be difficult to find and often must be created.

5-88. Topographic surveys can help determine the amount of usable area and the amount of work that needs to be accomplished to prepare a site selected for a combat outpost. Engineer support is often required for the removal of vegetation, rocks, and dirt and to clear, level, and prepare the site for construction. Leaders should plan for actions against enemy attacks targeted against friendly forces during the actual construction phase of the outpost.

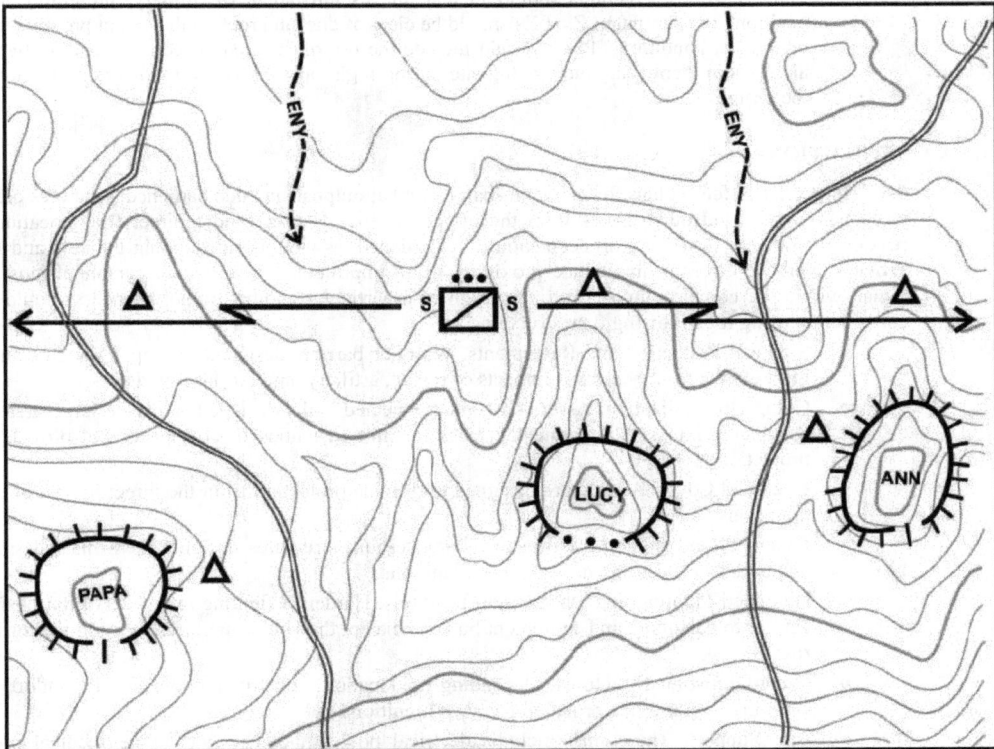

Figure 5-10. Combat outposts

5-89. Leaders should consider the following when establishing and conducting operations from a combat outpost:

- Mission. The site should be located in an area that adequately supports its mission.
- Security. The first priority is establishing all-around security, including patrols, OPs, and security plans during limited visibility.
- Protection. Select positions that provide, or can support construction of barriers that provides optimal protection from direct and indirect fires.
- Dispersion. A position and plan should not be established in such a way that it is vulnerable to bypass, isolation, and subsequent destruction from any direction.
- Fields of fire. Individual and crew-served weapons positions should plan for mutual support and fields of fire in all directions.
- Covered routes. If possible, the position should have at least one covered and concealed route that allows for resupply, medical evacuation, reinforcements, or withdrawal, and protection from direct fire weapons.
- Observation. Positions should permit observation of enemy avenues of approach and adjacent defensive sectors.
- Fire hazard. If possible, avoid selecting positions that are obvious fire hazards.
- Landing zones. Positions should include the establishment of primary, preferably inside the position, and alternate LZs. LZs should be clear of dust and rock to the extent possible to prevent brown out conditions. Plans should include the use of infrared beacons or landing lights to aid aircrews in identifying the landing site during night operations and to ensure a safe approach to the ground.

CONSTRUCTION

5-90. Integrated defense plans for mountain-based combat outposts include hardened structures designed to protect personnel and other assets from the effects of enemy direct and indirect fire. Locations where personnel routinely work, eat, or sleep should be hardened, as well as surrounding bunkers and foxholes. Provide overhead cover in immediate proximity to all unprotected areas where personnel must work or transit within the combat outpost. During design of a particular combat outpost, leaders should consider construction using the following type structures:

- Sidewall Protection and Revetments. Walls or barriers designed to stop fragments and reduce blast effects from near-miss impacts of rocket, artillery, and mortar rounds.
- Compartmentalization. A series of interconnected walls designed to divide large areas of high occupancy into smaller protected areas to limit casualties from impacts and provide ballistic protection.
- Overhead Cover. A structure designed to provide protection from the direct impact of incoming munitions.
- Personnel and Equipment Bunkers. Purpose-built structures designed to withstand small arms and both near miss and direct hits of munitions.
- Hardened Fighting and Observation Positions. Hardened fighting and observation positions are similar to personnel and equipment bunkers except they have apertures for returning or initiating fire.
- Use of Existing Structures. Depending on location, construction type, and standoff, existing structures can provide protection against munitions.
- Life Support. These may include electrical power, medical evacuation, medical provisions, hygiene facilities, waste plans, potable water, kitchen and mess area, rest and work out areas, heating and air conditioning, and phones and computers.

COMMAND AND CONTROL

5-91. The company or platoon CP for a combat outpost does not normally have a set organization. It consists of the commander or senior leader and other personnel and equipment required for supporting the C2 process and specific mission. The CP locates where the leader determines it can best support his C2 process. For a company-size combat outpost, the CP often consists of the commander and his radio-telephone operators, the fire support team headquarters, the communications NCO, the CBRN NCO, and the COIST. The XO, first sergeant, armorer, reserve element leader, and the leaders of attached or supporting units may also locate with the CP. CP personnel assist the commander in planning, coordinating, and issuing orders to support their mission. (For more on COIST operations see chapter 6 of this manual.)

COMMUNICATIONS

5-92. Combat outposts should have communication plans and networks to support their mission. They often have multiple means and backup means of communication for redundancy. During mountain operations, companies often operate on TACSAT radios to enhance communication efforts in the restrictive mountain terrain. As a minimum, combat outposts establish communications with higher, lower, adjacent, and supporting units. Combat outpost communications should be:

- Secure. The system should be able to restrict unauthorized monitoring and access to prevent information from being provided to unauthorized personnel. Leaders should insure that all systems meet guidance from higher commands regarding policies on encryption. Unauthorized personnel should not be allowed access to information over the systems.

- Robust. The systems should be able to withstand both the natural and manmade interference that may be in the area. For example, weather effects such as heat, cold, and rain can dramatically affect radio systems and this impact should be evaluated prior to establishing the systems. Man made factors such as interference created by urban areas, high tension power lines, commercial radio transmitters, cell phone towers and interference from radar and directional systems can impede communications and should be identified and factored into the plan prior to system establishment. Additionally, the system should be developed to withstand a single point of failure brought on by enemy attack.

- Redundant. To be robust, a system should have a duplicate and offer multiple links. Reliance on any single form of communication such as radio, telephone, or data probably does not support the commander's requirements. Every combat outpost should have a minimum of three alternate means of communications. Each should be properly identified as primary, secondary and tertiary that work as fail-safe systems in the event of a major attack or loss due to weather or interference. These three systems should be separate in type so as not to be impacted by the same event.

- Reliable. Systems should be dependable. Use of both commercial communications technology and Department of Defense-provided systems is the norm but each system and network should be researched as to its specific reliability. Systems with low mean time between failure or limited capabilities should not be relied on as key systems. Additionally, periodic and thorough maintenance of all systems should be directed and properly conducted to ensure system stability.

BASE DEFENSE PLANS AND ACTIONS

5-93. Base commanders, should establish a base defense SOP that outlines the base defense plan. (It should also include combat outposts.) They should disseminate the SOP down to the Soldier level, ensuring that every Soldier understands his part in the base defense plan. They should also conduct base defense exercises regularly to ensure compliance with the SOP. Along with many other details, plans should ensure they have procedures for:

- Establishing a base defense coordination net.
- Passing indications and warning to the unit CP and all personnel on the base.
- Raising force protection levels for all Soldiers on base.
- Activating and manning all perimeter supplemental positions.
- Reacting to/stopping a direct attack or perimeter breach by armed personnel.
- Reacting to IED incident.
- Reacting to attack from indirect fire or air attack; activating the bunker occupation plan.
- Reacting to/evacuating a casualty.

AIR ASSAULT

5-94. Air assault missions are a feasible option for combat missions in a mountain environment. Air assaults may be used in an independent operation or in conjunction with other offensive operations, such as an insertion of a unit to block a likely egress route for an enemy escaping another attacking force. Insertions are normally made by rotary-wing air assets to an LZ. In mountain environments, the enemy probably has observation on any aircraft including those used for an air assault. If the insertion is to be clandestine, leaders may have to take advantage of limited visibility conditions as well as other measures such as false insertions used for deception. The use of multiple aircraft can confuse the enemy on the actual location of the insertion. Primary and secondary LZs should be identified. Consideration should be given to how far the insertion point is to the objective keeping in mind that traversing long distances in the mountains on foot can quickly exhaust Soldiers. An extraction point for pick up after the operation should also be identified. (For more information on air assault operations see ATTP 3-18.12.)

5-95. Air assault operations in mountain terrain can be risky. If a larger enemy force than expected is encountered, reinforcements may not be readily available or may not be able to assist the unit in a timely manner. A main consideration for leaders planning an air assault mission in the mountains is the ever changing weather conditions. Many weather conditions can ground aircraft during any part of the operation. Adverse weather may cause the mission to be aborted or, if forces are already on the ground, alternative measures for extraction or exfiltration may have to be initiated.

TUNNELS AND CAVES

5-96. Tunnels, caves, and dry wells have historically been used for hiding places, food and weapons caches, headquarters complexes, and protection against air strikes and artillery fire. Enemy personnel use these areas for both offensive and defensive actions. An extensive tunnel system containing rooms for storage and hiding as well as passages to interconnected fighting points may be encountered. Tunnels and caves are not only a dangerous obstacle but also can be an outstanding source of enemy information. The presence of a tunnel complex within or near an area of operations poses a continuing threat to all personnel in the area and no area containing tunnel complexes should ever be considered completely cleared.

TUNNEL CHARACTERISTICS

5-97. The first characteristic of a typical tunnel complex is normally superb camouflage. Conceal entrances and exits and camouflage bunkers. Even within the tunnel complex itself, side tunnels may be concealed, trapdoors are often hidden, and dead-end tunnels are used to confuse the attacker. Air shafts are usually spaced at intervals throughout a tunnel system. In many instances, the first indication of a tunnel complex comes from direct fire received from a concealed bunker. Spoil from the tunnel system may be distributed over a wide area, giving clues to its existence.

5-98. Trapdoors may be used, both at entrances and exits and inside the tunnel complex itself, concealing side tunnels and intermediate sections of a main tunnel. In many cases, a trapdoor leads to a short change of direction or change of level tunnel, followed by a second trapdoor, a second change of direction, and a third trapdoor opening again into the main tunnel. Trapdoors may be of several types. They may be concrete covered by dirt, hard packed dirt reinforced by wire, or a "basin" type consisting of a frame filled with dirt. This last type is particularly difficult to locate in that probing may not reveal the presence of the trapdoor unless the outer frame is struck by the probe. Use booby traps extensively, both inside and outside entrance and exit trapdoors.

5-99. Tunnel complexes may also be interconnected with other tunnels, but concealed by trapdoors or blocked dirt passages that are up to three or four feet thick. Secret passages are usually known only to selected personnel and are used mainly in emergencies. Tunnels may also be interconnected by much longer passages through which relatively large bodies of men may be transferred from one area to another. The connectivity of these systems often allows the enemy to move unnoticed from one area to another, eluding friendly forces (Figure 5-11).

Figure 5-11. Tunnel system

5-100. Since tunnel complexes are carefully concealed and camouflaged, search and destroy operations should provide adequate time for a thorough search of an area to locate all tunnels. The use of local nationals and host nation scouts can be of great assistance in locating caves, tunnels, defensive positions, and likely ambush sites. Caves, trenches, spider holes, and tunnels are well incorporated into mountain terrain and enemy operations and may be used as a deception to draw friendly forces into a cave or tunnel system rigged with booby traps or set with an ambush.

DANGERS

5-101.   Considerations for dangers inherent in tunnel operations include—

- The presence of mines and booby traps in the entrance/exit area.
- The presence of small but dangerous concentrations of carbon monoxide produced by burning-type smoke grenades. (Protective masks can prevent inhalation of smoke particles but does not protect against carbon monoxide.)
- The possible shortage of oxygen as in any confined or poorly ventilated space.
- The possibility of the enemy still in the tunnel who pose a danger to friendly personnel both above and below ground. (In some instances, military working dogs can successfully detect enemy hiding in tunnels.)

PREPARATION FOR TUNNEL CLEARANCE

5-102.   Tunnels and caves are often outstanding sources of information and should be exploited to the maximum extent practicable. Complete exploitation and destruction of tunnel complexes is time consuming, and operational plans should be made accordingly to ensure success. Commanders may consider the use of thermobaric munitions for destruction of enemy personnel using tunnel systems. Thermobaric munitions are munitions that are intentionally optimized to create heat and pressure and designed to extend the pressure impulse time. These munitions create a cloud of volatile gases or powders which it ignites causing a fireball that consumes oxygen and creates an enormous overpressure. When employed in a tunnel, the blast wave or overpressure is greatly amplified resulting in catastrophic enemy personnel effects. Employment of thermobaric munitions may require coordination with a higher headquarters.

5-103.   A trained tunnel exploitation and denial team is essential to tunnel clearance operations. Untrained personnel may miss hidden tunnel entrances and caches, take unnecessary casualties from concealed mines and booby traps, and may not adequately deny the tunnel to future enemy use. Commanders should consider designating specific tunnel teams for clearance operations. Tunnel teams should be trained, equipped, and maintained in a ready status to provide immediate expert assistance when tunnels are discovered.

5-104.   Careful mapping of a tunnel complex may reveal other hidden entrances as well as the location of adjacent tunnel complexes and underground defensive systems. Personnel exploring large tunnel complexes should carry a colored smoke grenade to mark the location of additional entrances as they are found. Small caliber pistols are the weapons of choice in tunnels, since large caliber weapons without silencers may collapse sections of the tunnel when fired and damage eardrums. Constant communication between the tunnel and the surface is essential to facilitate tunnel mapping and exploitation. An equipment list for a tunnel team may include, but is not limited to, the following:

- Protective Mask - one per individual.
- Portable Blower - one each.
- TA-1 telephone - two each.
- M7A2 CS grenades - twelve each.
- One-half mile field wire on doughnut roll.
- Powdered CS-1 - as required.
- Compass - two each.
- Colored smoke grenades - four each.
- Sealed beam 12-volt flashlight - two each.
- Insect repellant and spray - four cans.
- Small caliber pistol with laser sight and white-light - two each.
- Technical mountaineering equipment (harness, headlamp) - one each.
- Entrenching tool - two each.
- Probing rods - 12 inches and 36 inches.
- Cargo packs on pack board - three each.
- Bayonet - two each.

Chapter 6

Augmenting Combat Power

Synchronization and coordination between all combat elements is key to successful mountain operations. Direct fires seldom are enough to achieve the desired effects on enemy targets in the mountains. In order to fully engage the enemy in mountain terrain, combined arms assets need to be employed. Offensive actions should be conducted with support from artillery or air assets and these fires should be initiated as soon as feasible to assist in the engagement. Artillery and air assets have the ability to reach into areas of defilade where direct fires cannot. Equally, effective offensive and defensive actions cannot be conducted without support from other sources such as intelligence, engineer, and sustainment assets.

REFERENCES

6-1. Table 6-1 consolidates the references to additional information.

Table 6-1. Guide for subjects referenced in text

Subject	References
Field Sanitation	FM 21-10
JFIRE, Multiservice Tactics, Techniques, and Procedures for the Joint Application of Firepower	FM 3-09.32
The Infantry Rifle Company	FM 3-21.10
Sniper Training	FM 3-22.10
Mountain Operations	FM 3-97.6
Military Mountaineering	FM 3-97.61
First Aid	FM 4-25.11
Unit Field Sanitation Team	FM 4-25.12
Basic Cold Weather Manual	FM 31-70
Altitude Acclimatization and Illness Management	TB MED 505
Heat Stress Control and Heat Casualty Management	TB MED 507
Prevention and Management of Cold Weather Injuries	TB MED 508
Company Intelligence Support Team	TC 2-19.63

INTELLIGENCE

6-2. The IPB products available to an Infantry company comes from the Battalion or Brigade S-2 and their staff. If those staffs had sufficient time to completely develop those products, they may contain sufficient detail to be of help in planning company and below small unit operations. These products may include the modified combined obstacle overlay, a battalion level terrain analysis product, that should contain information on mobility corridors down to platoon size. It may also include analysis of infiltration or exfiltration routes within the company AO. While these products are helpful, a detailed map and leader's reconnaissance remains essential to effective operations. To help organize, sort, and understand relevant intelligence related information, companies often employ a COIST.

COMPANY INTELLIGENCE SUPPORT TEAM

6-3. Infantry companies do not have an organic intelligence analysis element and the abundance of information gathered from various sources can quickly become overwhelming and unmanageable to a commander. Operations in Iraq and Afghanistan have shown that the company commander alone cannot effectively process all the intelligence related information received. In order to effectively perform their mission in those environments, leaders recognized the need for assistance in conducting intelligence related functions at the company level. That, along with other intelligence related activities that must be conducted at the company level, has resulted in the development of what many units now refer to as a COIST.

6-4. A company intelligence support team is an organization formed at the company level to perform intelligence tasks as directed by the commander. The COIST performs analysis, processing, and dissemination of tactical information and intelligence for the company commander. Commanders usually establish COISTs while conducting stability operations but may also establish COISTs to provide dedicated intelligence support during offensive or defensive operations. The need for a company intelligence team in no way negates the need for intelligence sections at higher echelons. The COIST is most effective if its work is complementary to that of the battalion S-2. (For more information on COIST see TC 2-19.63.)

COIST Functions

6-5. While commanders can have their team perform a number of different operations, typical functions the COIST conducts include—

- Processing company requirements.
- Identifying methods for accessing information from higher and adjacent units.
- Developing methods for performing analysis.
- Determining methods for input of information.
- Managing intelligence tasks.
- Managing reconnaissance and surveillance tasks.
- Displaying company information graphically to provide situational awareness.
- Reporting information to higher, lower, and adjacent units.

6-6. COIST operations include data collection. Data collection and consolidation into a database is an effective way to gain knowledge of the surrounding area and people. Routine patrolling by unit personnel can offer opportunities for data collection. Leaders should instruct personnel on what type of data they would like collected for later consolidation. By doing this, leaders and unit personnel have a better understanding of personnel in the area, who may be new, what type of actions they are performing, what may seem out of place, or what observations may be an indication of enemy activity.

COIST Tasks

6-7. COISTs perform two basic tasks for the commander: support to situation development and support to targeting (lethal and nonlethal). Within these two primary tasks, the COIST accomplishes numerous subtasks.

6-8. Support to situation development is analyzing information and producing current intelligence about the operational environment, enemy, terrain, and civil considerations before and during operations. Situation development helps the commander make decisions and execute branches and sequels. The process requires the COIST to refine information received on threat intentions, objectives, combat effectiveness, and potential missions in the company AO.

6-9. Support to targeting (lethal and nonlethal) is the task of providing the commander information and intelligence support for targeting through lethal and nonlethal actions. It includes intelligence support to planning and execution of the following:

- Direct and indirect fires.
- Information engagements.
- Electronic warfare.
- Assessment of those operations.

SIGNALS INTELLIGENCE

6-10. While detection of enemy forces in mountain environments is difficult through visual observation, detection through signals intelligence is extremely effective and accurate. Communications intelligence (COMINT) assets have been used extensively in mountain environments to locate the enemy from the point of origin of the signal, and to listen to the message traffic to help determine their intent and plans for enemy actions. A variety of detection systems exist and often some of these assets, or the intelligence derived from these assets, are available at the company and below level.

6-11. COMINT systems can not only be used to monitor for unexpected transmissions but also can be used in combination with a planned offensive operation by monitoring for expected transmissions in response to a friendly action. For example, a patrol conducted in mountain terrain should expect that they are being observed by enemy forces and that their movement into an area is detected. Using COMINT systems to actively monitor for subsequent enemy radio transmissions as a result of patrol movements can pinpoint a suspected location and orient patrol efforts. Message content may also determine enemy intent such as an ambush set up to intercept the patrol. This information to a leader is invaluable as it gives a location but a probable course of enemy action. The enemy at this stage loses the element of surprise and leaders can prepare for an organized response.

6-12. Air assets as well as ground movements can be used in the same manner to help locate enemy forces. Fixed- or rotary-wing assets can fly over or near an area to simply create radio communication traffic from enemy personnel which can be pinpointed through COMINT systems. Any unusual activity or deception measures that are likely to cause enemy personnel to transmit communications may be used in a similar manner.

EVERY SOLDIER A SENSOR

6-13. To ensure maximum combat effectiveness, Soldiers should master a diverse set of skills. On a battlefield fought among enemies that are difficult to recognize and that use nonconventional tactics, Soldiers should be keenly aware and astute to anomalies, changes, and other clues in the surrounding environment and populace that may signal danger or threats. The concept of ES2 is that Soldiers are indispensable sources for an abundance of information that can be used by intelligence assets. Observations and experiences of Soldiers provide depth and context to information gathered through surveillance and reconnaissance. Soldiers should report their observations, even when not assigned a surveillance or reconnaissance mission. Soldiers often work in and among the local populace and can read, sense, or detect abnormalities, inconsistencies, or irregularities in their behavior or actions. The same can be said about the environment in which the Solder operates. All Soldiers should look for anything that seems out of place or inconsistent with what is normally encountered and report their findings.

6-14. In mountain operations, information detected by Soldiers may be as simple as a pile of rocks that looks out of place or indigenous personnel acting strangely or overly curious as to the unit's actions. For example, mountain passes are prime locations for an ambush and sites may be enhanced with explosives to corral or confuse friendly units. An alert Soldier may detect a change or disturbance in the terrain from a previous mission which could indicate possible buried explosives. Populations often unintentionally give off clues to danger. Generally, local personnel gather in towns and villages, many being in lower lying areas. Soldiers may also encounter villages and populace in the mountains. Soldiers should remain vigilant and attentive to details about local personnel that may indicate possible enemy activity.

DIRECT AND INDIRECT FIRES

6-15. To gain maximum effectiveness, Soldiers and leaders should be thoroughly familiar with all weapons in their unit and with those that could support them. All the principles of direct and indirect fire control as discussed in FM 3-21.10 apply to mountain operations with special considerations as discussed below.

DIRECT FIRES

6-16. Common direct fire weapons for units operating in the mountains include rifles, machine guns, and grenade launchers. An Infantry platoon conducting a combat patrol in the mountains would have its organic weapons including the weapons squad MGs. Leaders determine whether to keep the weapons squad pure or to attach the MGs to specific squads during their mission.

6-17. Soldiers should confirm zero on all direct fire weapons upon arriving in the mountains to compensate for environmental differences along with any changes that occurred during transport. Whenever possible, units should re-zero their weapons after large changes in temperature or elevation. Maintaining an accurate zero is key for all Soldiers. Aim points may also need to be adjusted for wind or for firing at large angles.

Small Arms and Machine Guns

6-18. Engaging targets with direct fire in mountain terrain can be deceiving and frustrating unless personnel are at least generally familiar with the effects of bullet trajectory while shooting from and to different elevations. Many factors affect the trajectory of bullets in the mountains, including differences such as the decrease in atmospheric pressure. Weapon mounted optics are a valuable asset for mountain operations, especially in or near max range direct fire engagements, and can help compensate for these differences if used properly. Weapon mounted optics should be used whenever possible on both crew served and individual weapons.

6-19. During target engagements, aiming points for direct fire weapons, including all small arms and machine guns, may have to be adjusted depending on the angle of the target from the shooter. Angle shooting is the term used for engaging a target at a different elevation than the shooter. Angle shooting has an effect on the trajectory of the projectile. At close distances the affect is minimal. At further distances the effect can result in a target miss above the target unless the shooter compensates for the difference and aims low. This is true whether the target is at a higher elevation than the shooter or at a lower elevation than the shooter (Figure 6-1).

6-20. How far to hold below the target depends on the range and angle to the target. These effects can be accounted for if the range to the target is known fairly accurately. As range increases (beyond 400 meters) the effects can become noticeable and need to be accounted for. Without some type of range determining electronics, Soldiers often tend to overestimate the range to a distant target on an angle. Overestimation of these ranges may have the opposite effect and cause a shooter to miss high. As a rule of thumb, and without determining the exact range and amount of compensation needed, Soldiers should aim at the base of the target for any partially exposed target. For a fully exposed target aim point should be approximately at waist level. (For more information see FM 3-22.10.)

6-21. Wind can also be a major contributing factor in adjusting aim points to effectively engage targets. While wind at any elevation can be an issue when shooting long distances, mountain winds can be extremely strong and are often more constant than at lower elevations. Strong mountain winds can cause bullets to drift off the aim point significantly. Smoke in or near the engagement area can give some indication to direction and strength of wind currents to aid in aim point adjustments. Learning to adjust to these conditions takes some practice but leaders and Soldiers need to be aware of how these conditions affect their aim points in order to compensate for them.

Shoulder Launched Munitions/Close Combat Missiles

6-22. Shoulder launched munitions (SLMs) and CCMs can be effective in mountain operations but limiting factors often preclude them from use in higher level rugged terrain. While planning for the use of these systems in mountain operations, leaders need to consider that one of the main impacts they have on operations is their weight and the ability to carry them into mission area locations. Leaders have to determine the impact on Soldier strength and endurance as opposed to the advantage of having these weapons available for use. SLM and CCM systems can be bulky and cumbersome for dismounted operations in mountain terrain and can weigh between 8 and 18 pounds. These factors may lead leaders to preclude them from mountain patrols when compared to the probability of needing their employment. Consideration should be given to their usefulness on missions where few vehicles are able to travel. While the CLU can offer great optics for increased observation capabilities, its weight is also a consideration.

6-23. Other considerations may include systems such as the M141 bunker defeat munition for use against caves, tunnels, and fortified positions. These munitions may be an option as they are less bulky in the collapsed position and can be used to incapacitate the enemy in caves and tunnels. Leaders should determine whether use of these systems is warranted for each operation based on all factors of METT-TC.

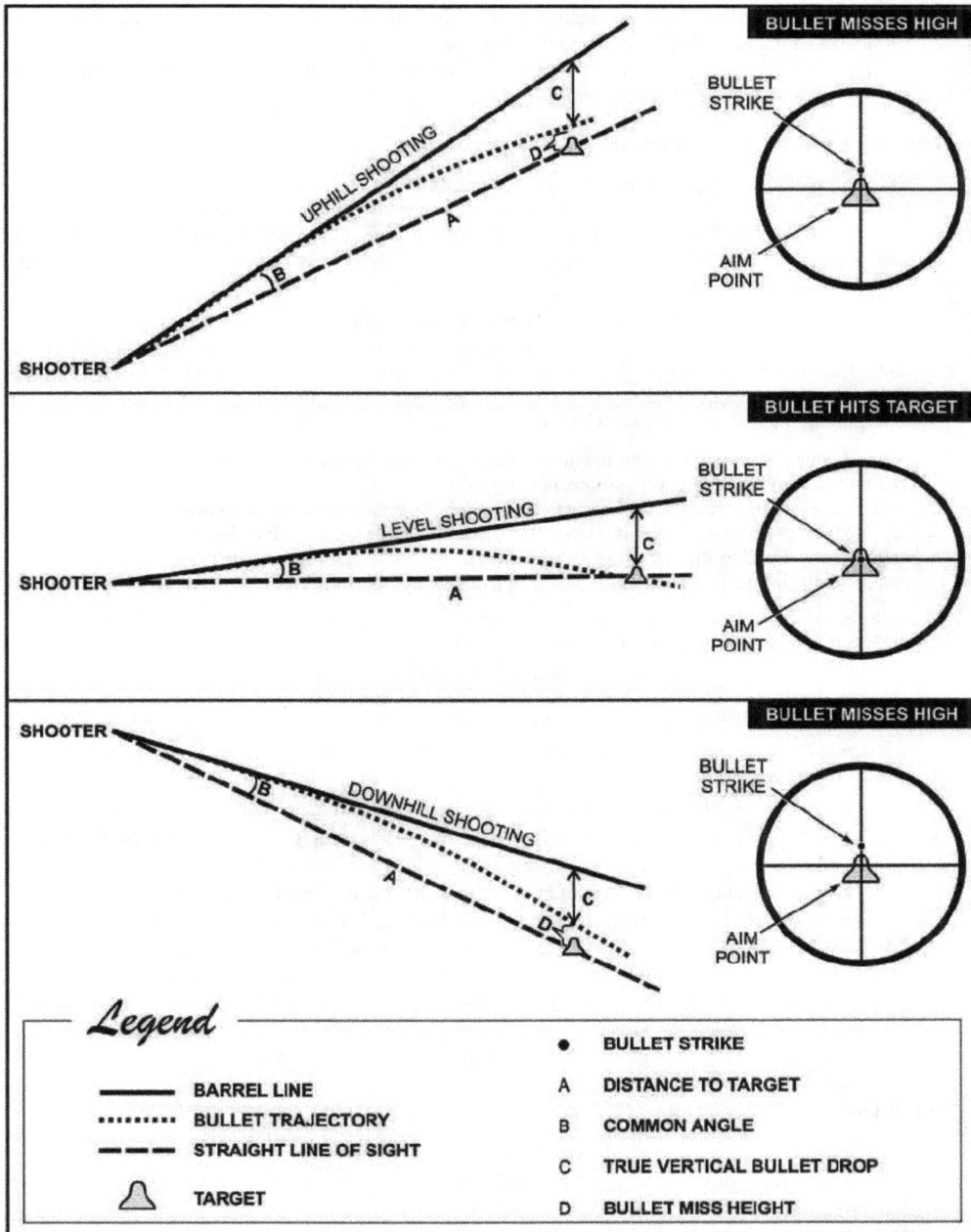

Figure 6-1. Angle shooting

6-24. SLMs and CCMs are effective weapons for integration into mountain terrain defensive positions. These systems are often placed covering likely main avenues of approach. They should be integrated into the plan with other direct fire weapons capitalizing on their unique capabilities. They have a longer range than other direct fire weapons and can have a much greater effect on targets hiding among the mountain rocks. Theses munitions have the capability of penetrating rocks and creating explosive debris unlike many small arms munitions. The Javelin and the ITAS are effective systems for long range engagements of hard targets. The CLU can also offer great optics for increased observation capabilities and may be used either in an OP or within a defensive position.

Snipers and Designated Marksmen

6-25. Snipers and designated marksmen should be employed to maximize their unique capabilities. Snipers particularly are trained specifically in observation techniques and are equipped with enhanced optics. They may be used as OP observers or positioned to cover a likely avenue of approach for a defensive position. They may also be positioned on a high point with 360-degree observation where they can observe as well as engage targets.

6-26. Snipers can give the unit leader the ability to interdict targets while providing real time reporting and warning. They can observe key terrain, engage with precision offensive or protective direct fire, and call and adjust indirect and aerial fires. In a mountain environment, snipers are an extremely valuable asset. Snipers should be equipped with items, such as laser rangefinders and cosign indicators to assist in determining the affects of angle on ballistics.

6-27. A sniper's unique training in camouflage, concealment, and movement also allows him to move into difficult or remote mountain positions undetected where he can observe, engage targets with direct fire, or coordinate for supporting fires. Snipers can be used for reconnaissance and surveillance. They may also be used for target acquisition feeding target locations to other assets, such as indirect and air assets, for target engagement. Finding the enemy in the mountains is a challenge for snipers as it is for any unit. It requires patience, discipline, and attention to detail. It often becomes a waiting game for the enemy to appear.

6-28. A critical step in the employment of snipers in a mountain terrain is the planning and preparation of the mission. Planning considerations should include—

- Developing a detailed terrain analysis and discussing any questions about the terrain and routes with personnel who have operated on that terrain. Maps may not always show smaller but still potentially dangerous terrain features.
- Using all available intelligence assets including satellite imagery, intelligence personnel, and unit personnel.
- Identifying historically high threat areas and potential attack locations and minefields.
- Avoiding areas where mobility is further decreased, such as in mud or deep snow, upon infiltration and exfiltration.
- Understanding the effects of temperature, altitude, and wind in the area.
- Equipping snipers with altimeters to take the guess work out of determining altitude.
- Masking movements in the mountains by staying in draws, staying off ridges, and mainly moving at night and observing during the day. Use of early morning mountain fog can also be used to obscure movements and insertions.
- Using night observation devices during movements at night.
- Considering all insertion means including air, vehicle, and foot.

Employment Considerations

6-29. Unique considerations for the employment of direct fires in mountain environments include—

- Using nonstandard shooting positions due to the steep angles often required for target engagement.
- Adjusting for limitations in the up or down angle of test and evaluation mechanisms for mounted or fixed weapon systems. Modification of existing mounts or placing sandbags under crew served weapons to elevate the weapon and engage targets at high angles may be necessary.
- Using plunging fires for direct fire weapons that are less effective in rocks, boulders, and defilade positions.
- Identifying acquired targets by using tracers to mark the area for other direct fires. Laser pointers and IR illuminators may also be used for the same purposes at night.

- Using the grenade launchers and grenade machine guns to fire into dead space and cover areas not possible with small arms.
- Carrying tripods on patrols to ensure accurate firing of MGs.
- Using hand-carried machine guns to fire on steep ridgelines close to the road or path where other heavy firepower systems are limited.
- Establishing target reference points on range cards for known distances in the mountains terrain where distances can be difficult to judge.
- Establishing wind indicators for unpredictable and constantly changing mountain winds. Indicators of wind strength and direction help determine where to aim direct fire weapons for effective engagements.

EMPLOYMENT OF INDIRECT FIRE

6-30. The ability for howitzers and mortars to engage targets on reverse slopes and areas of defilade is a tremendous advantage for mountain terrain combat. As with other operations, employing indirect fires in mountain terrain and climate does have its challenges. Unique challenges include—

- Unpredictable weather conditions that can affect the accuracy of the rounds.
- Targets located on peaks and steep terrain making adjustments difficult.
- Intervening crests requiring placement of observers on dominating heights for observation.
- Limited terrain suitable for firing positions to cover a particular mission.
- Artillery and mortar locations ideal for range and coverage unsuitable due to intervening mountain terrain features.
- Locations tactically positioned but in an area prone to avalanches or flash floods.
- Shifting artillery assets to alternate locations requiring significant engineering and logistical efforts.

Artillery Fires

6-31. Indirect fires are valuable assets in the mountains. High angle fires can assist in reaching into defilade positions and the combat power and destructiveness of artillery munitions has both a physical and psychologically traumatic effect on the enemy. High angle fires are often preferred in mountain terrain in order to engage targets in defilade. In addition, high angle fires are may be preferred for safety reasons. Low trajectory rounds fired into uneven, sloping, rocky terrain may have a tendency to skip and detonate in an unintended area. Leaders need to enforce the daily inspections of indirect fire systems as missions fired at max charge and high angle, both common in mountain engagements, are extremely hard on cannons and mortar base plates.

6-32. In mountain terrain, availability of firing positions may be limited. Road access may be restricted for both movement and resupply. Artillery positions require trafficable access into the sites if emplacement and resupply is by ground vehicles. Towed Howitzers may be air lifted by helicopter into positions. Units inserted by air should have adequate level positions and resupply areas as well. With automation capabilities, the guns need not be in one location but can be dispersed throughout the area. Positions often need to be configured for 360-degree firing as indirect fires may be required in any direction in mountain operations (Figure 6-2).

Figure 6-2. Mountain artillery firing

6-33. Steep mountain terrain creates challenges for adjusting and ensuring effective indirect fires. An artillery round affecting 50 meters away from the intended target on fairly level or close to level terrain may be effective while the same horizontal 50 meters in mountain terrain may cause the round to impact significantly above or below the target. Due to a steep mountain slope, the impact of these rounds may render no effect at all (Figure 6-3). Observers should be aware of this consequence and consider creeping rounds for adjustments to increase the probability of target effects. Creeping adjustment rounds from a lower elevation up to the target are often better since impacts over a ridgeline are difficult or impossible to observe.

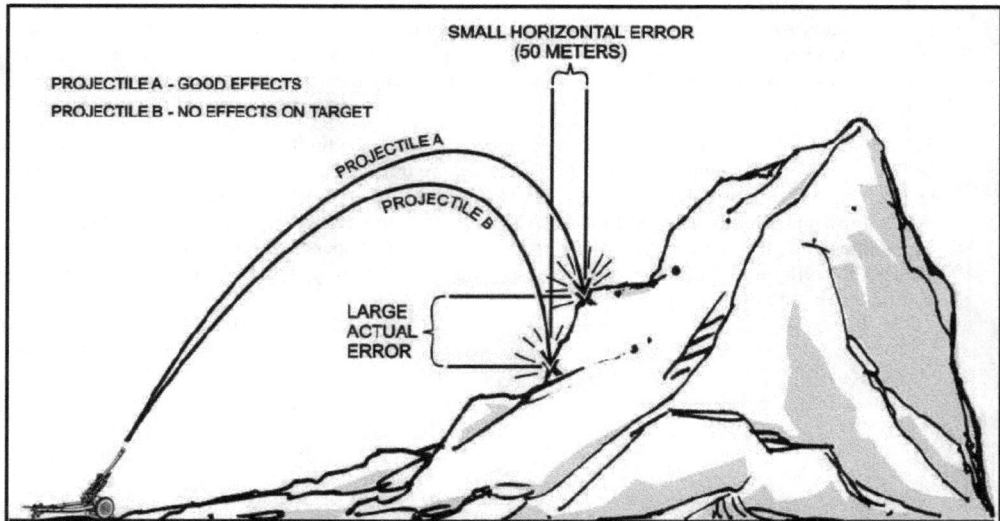

Figure 6-3. Mountain effects on artillery

Mortar Fires

6-34. Mortars are a tremendous asset in mountain operations. They are relatively easy to emplace in a mountain terrain and can be set up and moved quickly. By design, they are well suited for firing into defilade positions. Infantry company 60-mm mortars can be carried by personnel wherever dismounted movements are possible. These mortars are a readily available, quick response, indirect fire power asset for the company and can be fired in the direct lay or handheld mode. Battalion level mortars can be used to support company or smaller unit operations but often must be carried and emplaced using some sort of vehicle or other transportation asset. Resupply of ammunition to these mortars is somewhat easier to accomplish than resupply to a dismounted unit where vehicles cannot travel.

6-35. Mortar rounds are affected by terrain and meteorological conditions similar to artillery rounds. Artillery considerations can be applied to mortars as well, with the lighter rounds, less trajectory altitude, and shorter flight times accounting for differences in how mortar rounds vs. artillery rounds are affected. Meteorological (MET) data and registration when possible can increase accuracy of the mortars.

6-36. Company commanders may consider employing company mortars by keeping one with the main body and sending one with a platoon or squad on patrol. During dismounted operations, commanders must account for carrying mortar rounds as well as the system itself. Mortar rounds not used during the conduct of a dismounted mission should be recovered upon completion and carried back out.

6-37. Clearance of company mortar missions often remains at the company level which can aid in a quick fire mission response. An even quicker response is achieved by firing 60-mm mortars in the handheld, direct-lay mode. These quick mortar engagements can suppress enemy targets while the unit maneuvers. Rules of engagement, particularly concerning airspace clearance of indirect fires, should be adhered to in all instances.

6-38. Suitable firing positions for mortars can be a challenge to find, but are typically easier to locate than artillery positions. Once located, it can be extremely difficult to dig them into a rocky position. Mountain terrain often makes digging in a less feasible option than the alternative method of building up a mortar position which also creates some unique problems while firing. During a direct attack, the gunner must often expose himself to the enemy in order for him to see the aiming stakes from a built up position. One technique to alleviate this problem is to mark the inside walls of the built up mortar position with known directions or target reference points. In this way a gunner can traverse the mortar to a desired deflection without having to directly observe the aiming stakes.

6-39. Mortar positions are often established within the confines of a defensive position alleviating the need to provide separate security personnel in an already personnel constrained situation. As with artillery positions, mortars in defensive positions usually prepare to fire in all directions.

Employment Considerations

6-40. High angle fires can engage targets behind crests, in defilade, and other unobservable areas otherwise not targetable with direct fires. High explosive air bursts tend to be more effective than point-detonating rounds in mountain terrain. Point detonating rounds impacting in rocky areas may achieve good effects due to the addition of rock splinters but larger boulders may provide some protection from those splinters and shell fragments.

6-41. In winter, rounds impacting in deep snow may have a higher incidence of duds. Deep snow, as well as large rocks, can also reduce the radius of lethality for impact shell bursts. Airburst detonations help improve lethality. Proximity fuzes are often preferred in mountain terrain but in snow storms may give false reading causing rounds to detonate prematurely.

6-42. White phosphorus (WP) smoke may be used as a marking round for orienting direct fires and fires from aviation assets. Leaders should consider that using WP may be hard for pilots without thermal sights to see in snow. WP should be used cautiously in snow as pieces of WP may continue to burn for days if covered by snow. Colored smoke or near-surface illumination bursts may be used to mark targets for aircraft in conditions where snow is present.

6-43. Atmospheric conditions may significantly alter an indirect fire round's trajectory. The projectile may be affected by minor variations in wind, air density, air pressure, and air temperature from round to round. Current MET data and/or registration data need to be available to account for these and other meteorological conditions. Ballistic MET data with a valid registration mission helps ensure increased first round accuracy. Registration missions should be conducted at an elevation close to that of a planned mission. A large change in elevation often requires a new registration be conducted as the altitude difference can affect the accuracy.

6-44. Precision munitions such as the guided multiple launch rocket system missiles or the 155-mm Excalibur round are effective in engaging precisely located targets. These global positioning system (GPS) assisted rounds can correct for unanticipated meteorological conditions in the target area.

6-45. Mountain operations may require the firing of danger close missions to engage targets in close battles. Meteorological data should be updated as frequently as possible to increase accuracy.

6-46. Commanders should consider targeting likely and previously used enemy firing positions that have been identified. The enemy may establish a pattern or reuse firing points and calculated data to those targets can provide for rapid counterfire.

EMPLOYMENT OF AIR ASSETS

6-47. Aircraft can attack targets that cannot be effectively engaged with other systems in mountain environments. The two major limiting factors for aircraft is their availability and the restrictions placed on their employment due to terrain and weather conditions. While coordination, deconfliction, and the use of air space and air corridors are accomplished at higher levels of command, company commanders should be aware of how mountain terrain and other restrictions may affect the use of air assets for their operations. For example, high mountain ridgelines that create a natural air avenue of approach may restrict friendly air assets from attacking enemy targets on a perpendicular axis to the friendly attacking ground force. This may force air assets to engage targets on a parallel axis to the moving ground unit creating additional control measures or visual signals to assist in marking the location of friendly forces.

6-48. Aviation platforms are excellent assets for attacking and fixing enemy personnel in position. The mere presence of fixed or rotary-wing aircraft flying in or near an enemy position is often enough to keep them from moving and exposing them to devastating fires. Enemy personnel operating in mountain terrain may be extremely reluctant to leave their positions if aircraft are flying overhead for fear of being seen or attacked.

6-49. The use of aircraft can be used in a preplanned offensive operation for friendly forces seeking an engagement. Aircraft can assist in a planned operation by loitering outside of sight and sound of a known or suspected enemy position until contact is made. Once contact is made, the on-call aircraft can quickly move on station to fix, hold, or attack enemy personnel for combined arms offensive actions. This technique creates a situation where enemy personnel are more willing to initially engage friendly units and expose their position than if the aircraft were visible in the area at the start of the mission.

Close Combat Attack

6-50. Attack reconnaissance aircraft can be extremely useful in the mountains and are often used to conduct close combat attacks (CCA) in support of ground forces. Helicopters can effectively engage targets hiding in rugged mountain terrain too difficult to quickly reach by foot and can assist ground forces in target location and target engagements. Final coordination for actual CCA engagements should be through direct voice communications between the aircraft and the supported unit. Attack helicopters can change to the company command net for direct communications where leaders can then direct them onto an exact target. CCA check-in format and CCA briefing format can be found in FM 3-09.32.

6-51. Some sort of terrain feature or other means of marking the target is often used as reference for locating a target for the pilot. Mortar WP rounds, visible to both the aircraft and the unit can mark a target or establish a reference point for guiding pilots onto targets. If mortars are not available, aircraft are often able to mark a target grid with aircraft delivered WP. Ground units can then refine corrections onto the target using the marking round for reference. If the target is within range of grenade launchers, colored smoke marking rounds may also be used.

6-52. In a defensive engagement, the response time for attack reconnaissance aircraft is affected by the availability of aircraft and the distance to the unit under attack. In a particular AO, the enemy may learn from repeated engagements approximately how long it takes for air assets to arrive once they attack a unit and plan their actions accordingly. They may try to cease their attack before or when friendly air assets arrive. They may also attempt to conduct their operations during conditions where air assets are grounded or hampered by limited visibility.

6-53. Attack reconnaissance aircraft may also be used as a show of force to discourage enemy units from performing offensive actions. Coordination can be made with any aircraft conducting nearby operations to simply fly over or near a planned company movement to deter aggressive actions and ambushes.

6-54. Major limitations for the use of attack reconnaissance aircraft include—

- The number of aircraft available. Sorties are often limited and in high demand in mountain operations.
- The time needed to get the aircraft on station. Available aircraft may be too far away or have to take a lengthy indirect route to be effective.
- Weather conditions. Current or pending weather conditions may ground the aircraft.
- Elevation restrictions. High mountain ridges may be at an elevation that restricts movement of rotary-wing aircraft across them. Simply getting the aircraft to a target area may be restricted if available aircraft are on the other side of the mountains with ridges above a certain altitude.
- Rearming and refueling. Travel time to many locations may be lengthy and use a substantial amount of fuel. This reduces time on station for the aircraft and requires refueling. Locations for rearming and refueling may also be some distance away.

Close Air Support

6-55. CAS may be made accessible for support to small-unit operations depending on the nature of the mission and the availability of aircraft. As with CCA missions, final coordination for CAS missions should be conducted with direct voice communications between the aircraft and the supported unit through a qualified Joint Terminal Attack Controller (JTAC) during terminal control procedures. CAS missions can be conducted using a non-JTAC certified individual, but must be clearly stated to aircraft as such. This alerts the aircrew to be prepared to "PULL" information to complete the critical portions of the CAS briefing. CAS check-in format and CAS 9-line briefing format can be found in FM 3-09.32.

6-56. Mountain terrain can all look similar and often some type of marking system is often needed to help identify targets. As with attack reconnaissance aircraft, some CAS platforms, such as the A10, can deliver WP munitions to use as reference points.

6-57. Fixed-wing platforms, such as A10s and F16s, may also be used as a show of force to discourage enemy units from conducting offensive actions. Ground units not wishing to make contact with the enemy may use fixed-wing assets to discourage enemy actions just by their mere presence. Since CAS is often a planned mission with coordination accomplished many hours or days in advance, the availability of assets to aid in defending a position from a surprise attack may be delayed. Aircraft used in these circumstances is often diverted from another mission. (See FM 3-09.32 for additional information on the employment of CAS.)

6-58. Mountain terrain may restrict effective CAS engagements. Pilots select a suitable approach route to the target area in the event a non-JTAC qualified controller is conducting the request. Targets may not be clearly visible to fast-moving aircraft due the terrain itself, climate and weather conditions, or a combination of both. Enemy personnel and equipment can hide among the rocks and in cracks, crevices, and draws. Those same features can create dark shadows on targets depending upon the time of day. Target identification for CAS missions can be enhanced through the use of lasers or smoke for marking enemy positions.

6-59. Mountain weather conditions may restrict fixed-wing aircraft from flying at all or may create a situation where aircraft personnel cannot see or find the target. Climate conditions that often affect aircraft include clouds, heavy rain, snow, dense fog, and gusting winds.

PROTECTION

6-60. Engineer support is often required to assist in protection measures by construction and hardening of positions in mountain operations. Engineers can turn a piece of rocky, hard, and uneven terrain into a suitable location for the establishment of a base or an LZ. They are often required to perform duties during construction of a hardened position and other vertical or horizontal construction efforts and have the heavy duty equipment to clear areas and lift heavy construction materials. Established operating bases such as a combat outpost have increased protection from direct and indirect fires through the construction of berms, barriers, fences, control points, guard towers, waste management facilities, and compound walls and overhead cover emplaced by engineers. (For more information on combat outposts see Chapter 5 of this manual.)

6-61. Infantry companies operating in mountain environments employ passive and active air defense measures to reduce the effectiveness of enemy attack or surveillance by enemy aircraft, UAS, or missiles. Passive air defense measures reduce the possibility of attack by making the company a less detectable target. Air defense artillery assets may be positioned in or near Infantry companies operating in mountain environments to aid in defense from air attacks. Passive air defense measures include—

- Using cover and concealment for stationary vehicles.
- Using camouflage to conceal reflective surfaces.
- Using covered and concealed routes during movement.
- Using cover and concealment at temporary stops and positions.
- Using prepared positions when possible.
- Not engaging passing aircraft unless it assumes an attack profile.
- Establishing air guards and an air warning system.
- Establishing immediate action drills.

SUSTAINMENT

6-62. Sustainment in a mountain environment is one of the biggest challenges to leaders and is often a difficult and time-consuming process. In mountain environments the company must often battle terrain and weather conditions as well as the enemy, complicating logistics resupply, medical and casualty evacuation, and Soldier health and hygiene.

EFFECTS ON PERSONNEL

6-63. Practically every aspect of mountain operations is affected more than if the same operations were conducted at lower altitudes in more forgiving terrain and weather conditions. Major conditions facing Soldiers conducting mountain operations include—

- Dismounted operations with heavy loads in rugged unforgiving terrain.
- Physical effects of high altitudes.
- Temperatures that vary from extremely hot to extremely cold.
- Rapidly changing weather conditions that may include violent storms.

Soldier's load

6-64. Soldier's load is a leadership responsibility regardless of the operating environment. Mountain terrain taxes Soldier strength and tests their endurance even more, making the scrutiny of Soldier load even tighter. Even though conditions experienced during mountain operations are more difficult than in more forgiving terrain and climate conditions, Soldiers are often required to increase their load as opposed to decrease it.

6-65. The fighting capability of an Infantry Soldier is directly related to his load. There is a maximum individual load limit that cannot safely be exceeded if an Infantry Soldier is expected to accomplish his combat mission. Commanders should consider the following points during Soldier load planning:

- The weight a Soldier can carry is based on his weight, the climate, the terrain, and the stress he has faced or is currently facing. Heavy loads, mountain terrain, high altitude, and extremely hot or cold weather all combine to sap a Soldier's strength.

- Each mission requires an analysis of the essential items that are necessary for survival and combat operations, including environment, weather, mission purpose and duration, Soldier requirements prior to initiating the mission, and definitive items that compose the Soldier's load.

- Combat loads in the mountains tend to be stripped as much as possible. Decisions on items such as the amount of food and water taken as well as the configuration of body armor should be determined in cutting weight from the combat load.

- While assault packs vary by role or function within the unit, leaders determine their exact contents. To assist in managing Soldier load, leaders may consider using the acronym DROP; D – decide mobility level, R – reduce unnecessary gear, O – organize resupply methods, P – police the ranks (inspect).

- For planning purposes, the fighting load for a properly-conditioned Soldier should not exceed 48 pounds, and the approach march load should not exceed 72 pounds including all clothing and equipment, either worn or carried.

- Overloading the Soldier can expose him to extreme risk. Unit SOPs should limit what is carried on combat operations and enforce those limits.

- The leader's involvement in analyzing the Soldier's load and the level of risk involved is the key to determining what is mission essential.

- Mountain terrain is usually rocky making it easy to twist an ankle or otherwise have a minor to moderate lower body injury with heavy loads. Injuries tend to increase in the winter due to the water, snow, and ice.

- Vehicles are not always available in the mountains to carry ammunition, food, and equipment, but should be considered for use whenever practical.

- Even in the most benevolent terrain, fatigue can become an issue. With rough mountain terrain and bad weather, the effects of fatigue multiply exponentially. Without proper rest, fatigue can greatly reduce the effectiveness of an otherwise highly trained unit.

- While season, climate, and weather conditions impact on items carried in mountain operations, Soldiers should be equipped for sudden weather changes as is characteristic of mountain environments.

- Contingency plans for additional supplies should be made, including a means for purifying mountain spring or stream water if needed.

- Inexperienced or new Soldiers to mountain operations may attempt to pack and carry more equipment than needed increasing the physical strain on their body and exhausting them more quickly. This not only impacts individual performance but also unit performance as well.

Acclimatization of Personnel

6-66. The immediate effect of high altitude on personnel is increased breathing and heart rate. This contributes to a perceived increase in exertion and shortness of breath. In simple terms, each breath an individual takes at a high altitude has less oxygen in it than at a low altitude. The reduction in available oxygen decreases a Soldiers' ability to adequately function. Tasks, requiring moderate to high exertion for several minutes or longer become harder to sustain and fatigue develops more quickly. Recovery from physical fatigue is slower. At high altitudes above 3,000 meters (10,000 feet), vision and judgment are impaired and sleep becomes irregular. Over some period an individual can improve their function by becoming "acclimatized" to the environment. Acclimatization allows for extended operations at high altitudes.

6-67. While all Soldiers should maintain a high standard of physical readiness and conditioning, troops scheduled to conduct operations at high altitudes should endure an acclimatization process in order to be effective and help prevent associated high altitude (HA) injuries. Mountain-warfare training is not a substitute for the acclimatization process. While stateside acclimatization is possible, deacclimatization is likely if transport times to theater exceed more than a few days and troops must acclimate in theater.

6-68. Acclimatization is required before undertaking extensive military operations. The expectation that freshly deployed, non-acclimated troops can go immediately into action is unrealistic and could be dangerous. Even the most physically ready Soldier experiences physiological and psychological degradation when thrust into high elevations. Time should be allocated for acclimatization, conditioning, and training of Soldiers. There is no shortcut for the acclimatization process and any attempt to trim or bypass the process usually results in personnel injuries. The duration of the acclimatization process depends on the altitude at which the unit must operate. Troops continue to train during the acclimatization process. Components of the acclimatization process and training include crossing crevasses, route marches, weapons firing, and rock climbing.

6-69. As a general rule most Soldiers can operate in mountains up to 2400 meters (8000 feet) with minimal effects, others may take more time to compensate. Acclimatization for mountain operations between 2400 and 4200 meters (8000 and 13800 feet) usually takes about 1 to 2 weeks on average and for operations above 4200 meters another 2 weeks is recommended. Acclimatization for higher altitudes is lengthy and rigid and cannot be shortened without serious consequences. Acclimatization for altitudes above 5200 meters (17000 feet) is generally not possible for many personnel but ground troops rarely operate at these heights.

Altitude Sickness

6-70. High altitudes can also cause altitude sickness. Altitude sickness is caused by body fluids leaking from the blood vessels into the tissues. Most affected are the brain and lungs. The most common altitude sickness is acute mountain sickness (AMS). AMS symptoms are headache, nausea, vomiting, dizziness, fatigue and sleep disturbances. AMS is common (over 20% incidence) above 2400 meters (8,000 feet) and both the incidence and symptom severity increases with higher altitudes.

6-71. In addition to AMS, the much less frequent but potentially life-threatening altitude sicknesses include high-altitude pulmonary edema (HAPE) and high-altitude cerebral edema (HACE). Symptoms of HAPE include severe shortness of breath, frothing at the mouth and cyanosis (blue color of skin). HACE symptoms include severe headache, stumbling, confusion, and incoherent speech.

6-72. All leaders and Soldiers should be aware of physical and mental changes in personnel that may be symptomatic of these illnesses. The most effective treatment for all altitude sickness is descent and rest. Soldiers well acclimatized to high altitudes are less susceptible to developing altitude sickness. (For more information see FM 3-97.6 and TB MED 505.)

6-73. During mountain operations, leaders should consider the following in relation to the effects altitude may have on Soldiers.

- Low altitude.
  - 0-1000 meters (0-3300 feet).
  - No effect.
- Moderate altitude.
  - 1000-2400 meters (3300-8000 feet).
  - Little to no effect.
  - Effects on Soldiers usually start around 2400 meters (8000 feet).
- High altitude.
  - 2400-4,200 meters (8000-14,000 feet).
  - Slower movement/performance.
  - Judgment and cognitive skills may be affected.
  - AMS (symptoms such as headache, nausea and dizziness).

- 300 meters (1,000 feet) per day above 3000 meters (10,000 feet) to acclimatize.
- Mandatory and immediate evacuation for HAPE, HACE 3700 meters + (12,000 feet +).
- 50-80% ineffective at 4200 meters (14,000 feet) from sea level.
- Very High altitude.
  - 4,200-6,000 meters (14,000- 19,800 feet).
  - Mandatory acclimatization (1-2 days for every 1,000 feet above 10,000 feet).
  - HAPE/HACE increase in severity and incidence.
  - Limited time at elevation (deterioration).
  - Highly experienced and trained personnel.
  - Specialized equipment.
- Extremely High altitude.
  - Above 6000 meters (19,800 feet).
  - Weeks of acclimatization.
  - No air assets above 5500 meters (18,000 feet).
  - Highly experienced and trained personnel.
  - Specialized equipment.

Temperature Effects

6-74. With high elevations also come colder temperatures. Temperature and humidity decrease with increasing altitude. As the body becomes accustomed to the cold temperatures, Soldiers can also become more adapted and efficient in functioning in a cold environment. Cold injuries, both freezing and nonfreezing, are generally the greatest threat at high altitudes. Frostbite and snow blindness are common injuries associated with the cold. Exertion causes the body to sweat which, in very cold temperatures, can freeze and possibly result in frostbite. Reviewing cold weather injury prevention, training in shelter construction, dressing in layers, and using the buddy system are critical and may preclude large numbers of debilitating injuries. The four essential requirements for survival in cold weather include:

- Warmth.
- Food.
- Water.
- Shelter.

6-75. Altitude sickness and cold injuries can occur simultaneously, with signs and symptoms being confused with each other. Coughing, stumbling individuals should be immediately evacuated to medical support at lower levels to determine their medical condition. Likewise, Soldiers in extreme pain from cold injuries who do not respond to normal pain medications, require evacuation. Without constant vigilance, cold injuries may significantly limit the number of deployable troops and drastically reduce combat power. With command emphasis and proper equipment, clothing, and training, the vast majority of cold-weather injuries are preventable. (For more information on cold injury causes, symptoms, treatment, and prevention see FM 31-70 and FM 4-25.11.)

6-76. Sun, heat and warmer weather in the mountains can also be a cause of injury. Atmospheric conditions make it easier for personnel to get sunburned. Warmer temperatures can also melt snow and create snow slides or avalanches. Heat related injuries can be found in the mountains especially among Soldiers conducting long term strenuous activities such as climbing with heavy loads. These type intense physical activities in the summer months, in direct sunlight, on hot humid days can increase the body's internal temperature. At some point, the body may lose its ability to get rid of the excess heat in order to compensate for these increases. When this happens, dehydration, heat exhaustion, or heat stroke may occur. (For more information on these type illnesses see FM 4-25.11.)

6-77. Leaders need to be aware of the symptoms that characterize a unit having difficulty coping with the extreme temperatures. The following considerations can help combat the effects of extreme temperatures when it begins to affect the minds of Soldiers:

- If Soldiers find it hard to remember things they have been taught, show patience; review orders and drills. Get them to think through the challenges of the environment and the mission; encourage them to ask questions. Keep their minds busy.
- Be alert for Soldiers who tend to withdraw from the group's focus; keep them involved. Soldiers who withdraw into themselves should be paired in a buddy system with Soldiers who are well acclimatized to the environment. Remind them that everyone is in the same situation, including the enemy.
- If Soldiers get depressed, moody, or blue, and do not want to talk, encourage them to chat with each other. Circulate among the troops in their duty areas. Keep them talking and interacting.
- If Soldiers become irritable and get on each other's nerves, keep in mind that this is likely to happen. Maintain your sense of humor and show patience. Vary their duties.
- Be aware that Soldiers may tend to shirk from some tasks. Remind them that their job is to fight and that weapons and equipment should be kept in fighting order.
- Do not accept the temperature as an excuse for not carrying out routine tasks. It may be the reason for taking longer, but it is not a reason for letting things slide. Remember that, although the extremely cold or hot temperatures may make tasks more difficult to accomplish, it does not make them impossible.
- Plan the frequent rotation of Soldiers into warming tents/areas to provide relief from the cold and provide warm liquids (noncaffeine) at frequent intervals.
- Ensure Soldiers remain hydrated both in cold and hot temperatures.
- Plan and provide extra insulating material for individuals, when available.
- As a general rule, leaders need to add an additional 1/3 of the normal time needed to any task performed in extreme cold weather from starting vehicles to operating weapons.

6-78. Leaders should routinely check Soldiers to enforce procedures for preventing temperature-related injuries. For a thorough explanation of heat- and cold-related injuries see FM 3-97.61, TB MED 507, and TB MED 508. Common heat and cold weather injuries include the following:

- Heat injuries.
  - Heat cramps.
  - Heat exhaustion.
  - Heat stroke.
  - Sunburn.
  - Dehydration.
- Cold weather injuries.
  - Hypothermia.
  - Frostbite.
  - Chilblain.
  - Immersion syndrome.
  - Snow blindness.
  - Sunburn.
  - Dehydration.
  - Constipation.
  - Carbon monoxide (CO) poisoning.
  - Tent eye.

Individual Equipment

6-79. Additional specialized equipment for individual Soldiers is often necessary and available for units deploying to mountain environments.

Cold Weather Clothing and Footwear

6-80. In addition to standard clothing issue for Soldiers, two versions of the extended cold weather clothing system Generation II and Generation III are available. These systems consist of three layers including a base layer, an insulation layer, and an outer shell. The base layer (also known as inner or wicking layers) is the layer adjacent to the body. These layers should be comfortably loose. The main purpose of these garments is to wick excess moisture away from the body. Insulation layers are the intermediate layers between the base and the outer shell. They provide volume to trap warm air between the body and the outer garments. They too help wick away excess moisture and should also be comfortably loose to trap a sufficient volume of air. The outer shell is the external layer that provides protection from precipitation and wind. In addition, it provides additional volume for trapping warm air. (For additional information on these systems see FM 31-70.)

6-81. Many Soldiers prefer commercially obtained boots for mountain operations. Using boots with specialized tread designs that are engineered for climbing and traversing rough terrain have become a standard practice for many units. Future developments for the Army are likely to include improved Mountain Combat Boots that have specialized tread and increased ankle stability for Soldiers deploying to mountain environments. Other types of equipment such as strap on foot traction devices to aid in movement across ice and snow are also available.

6-82. The design principles of the military cold weather clothing system are—
- Insulate. Insulation allows the creation of a microclimate around the body through which the amount of body heat lost to the environment can be regulated. By varying the amount of insulation, a Soldier can regulate the amount of heat lost or retained.
- Layer. Several layers of clothing provide more insulation and flexibility than one heavy garment, even if the heavy garment is as thick as the combined layers. By adding or removing layers of clothing (insulation), the Soldier can regulate the amount of heat lost or retained.
- Ventilate. Ventilation helps maintain a comfortable microclimate around the body, thereby helping control body temperature. By ventilating, the Soldier can release excess heat and minimize sweating, which can lower body temperature later as it evaporates.

6-83. The military principles for cold weather clothing system operations may be remembered by the acronym COLD-R as follows:
- Clean. Keep it Clean. Dirt and grease clog the air spaces in clothing and reduce the insulating effect. Dirty clothes are cold clothes.
- Overheating. Avoid overheating. Select the clothing needed to stay comfortable, or even a little cool. Leaders should ensure that their Soldiers are not overdressed for the job they are performing.
- Loose. Wear it loose in layers. All items of the cold weather uniform are sized to allow wearing of the appropriate number of layers. This means, for example, that the field jacket may appear too large when worn without all of the layers designed to fit under it. If the uniform items do not fit loosely, the insulation is substantially reduced.
- Dry. Keep it dry. It is vital that all layers of clothing be kept dry because wet clothing conducts heat away from the body, compromising the microclimate around the body and making it difficult to regulate body temperature. Moisture soaks into clothing from two directions: from melting snow and frost that has collected on the outside of the clothing and from perspiration. Leaders should ensure that Soldiers brush snow and frost from clothing before entering heated shelters or vehicles.
- Repair and replace. Repair damaged clothing and replace non repairable or nonfunctioning gear. Soldiers should constantly inspect their clothing for serviceability and repair or replace items as necessary.

Altimeters

6-84. Some personnel within the unit should have an altimeter and one should accompany every patrol in mountain environments. Leaders should be aware of their altitude in the mountains for both medical and operational reasons. Medical personnel may be a viable option for carrying altimeters as they can periodically keep a check on the unit's altitude as they traverse the mountain terrain. Altimeters can also be useful during route planning and during land navigation.

Water Purification Devices

6-85. Soldiers need plenty of fluids while conducting mountain operations. The amount of water needed for sustainment can be a heavy load to carry. Purification devices can render mountain water safe for consumption and may include purification tablets, MIOX pens, and water pump filters.

6-86. Hand held water treatment devices provide a means to aid in the production of potable water in short-term and emergency use situations. The type of hand held device should be selected after applying the principles of risk management, to include factors such as quality of the water to be treated, the duration of the mission, and the potential for existing and intentional contamination. Hand held water treatment devices are not a foolproof method of providing potable water and certain precautions should be taken in their selection and use. While these devices provide a certain level of treatment, the disinfection of the product water is often overlooked. A two-stage process of mechanical filtration with a hand held device, followed by chemical disinfection, is recommended for short-term and emergency use situations. In all cases, Army units should follow the manufacturer instructions for care and maintenance of the hand held treatment devices.

Individual Survival Items

6-87. Leaders also need to prepare Soldiers for unexpected and extended separations while conducting operations in the mountains. Enemy actions, weather conditions, or other circumstances may demand Soldiers or units to survive for some period in the mountains without external support. All personnel should be prepared for these situations. Although leaders determine what items will be carried by their Soldiers, the following list of common survival items is provided for consideration:
- Waterproof matches and fire starters (candles, magnesium match).
- Wire saw.
- Signaling devices (mirror, cold weather whistle).
- Pocket knife.
- Pressure bandage, lip balm, sunglasses.
- Water container (metal for use in fire).
- Compass.
- Emergency rations.
- Foil survival blanket.
- 5 meters of strong nylon cord or survival snaring wire.
- Small flashlight or headlamp.
- IR strobe.
- Potable water.

Nutrition

6-88. Soldiers require an increase in calorie and fluid intake in higher altitudes. A diet high in carbohydrates is important in helping the body fight the effects of these conditions. Fats provide long-term, slow caloric release but they are often unpalatable to Soldiers operating at higher altitudes. Snacking on high-carbohydrate foods is often the best way to maintain the calories necessary to function.

6-89. Weight loss is characteristic of operations at high altitude that Soldiers should closely monitor. The average weight loss for a Special Forces team working with the high-altitude mountain school was 20 to 25 pounds while living on Pakistani rations. Their schedule included 6 days of activity, 12 hours a day. Just moving around created above normal exertion. The bottom line in working at this altitude is that personnel are going to lose weight. Weight loss should be controlled before it becomes incapacitating. Weight loss leads to fatigue, loss of strength, and psychological changes, such as decreased mental capacity and alertness, and low morale. All of these conditions can contribute to accidents and a failure to accomplish the mission.

6-90. To help guard against issues associated with potential weight loss Soldiers should—

- Eat a high-complex carbohydrate diet, eating portions of the complete ration verses one item or the other.
- Eat at least one hot meal a day, using whatever heat source is available such as chemical heat packs, or other warming methods.
- Eat a variety of foods and snacks.
- Drink 4-6 quarts of non-caffeinated beverages a day. Caffeinated beverages can be consumed in moderation. Monitor the color and volume of urine for possible dehydration (dark yellow means take action).
- Not skip meals, even in the absence of appetite. Consume a little of everything in the ration.
- Not eat high fat snacks or fatty foods or consume alcohol of any type.
- Not force feed. This can result in vomiting and make the situation much more hazardous.
- Not drink unpurified water or melted snow. If melting snow for drinking purposes, ensure it is brought to a boil or purified by other means before drinking.
- Not restrict water intake to save it for later, or attempt to avoid urinating.

6-91. Significant body water is lost at higher elevations from rapid breathing, perspiration, and urination. In cold climates sweat, normally an indicator of loss of fluid, goes unnoticed. Sweat can evaporate so rapidly or be absorbed so thoroughly by clothing layers that it is not readily apparent. Thirst is not a good indicator of the amount of water lost. When Soldiers become thirsty, they may be already dehydrated. Dehydration increases the risk of developing acute mountain sickness (AMS), cold injuries, and physical fatigue.

6-92. To combat dehydration issues, Soldiers should consume about 4 to 8 quarts of water or other decaffeinated fluids per day in low mountains and may need 10 quarts or more per day in high mountains depending on level of exertion. Forced drinking in the absence of thirst, monitoring the deepness of the yellow hue in the urine, and watching for behavioral symptoms common to AMS are important factors for commanders to consider in assessing the water balance of Soldiers operating in the mountains.

6-93. Canteens should be filled as often as possible and units should carry means to purify and disinfect mountain ground water. Leaders should consider the use of commercial water purification systems to reduce the amount of water carried by individuals. Careful consideration should be given to the type of hand held device. Decision should be selected after applying the principles of risk management, to include factors such as quality of the water to be treated, the duration of the mission, and the potential for existing and intentional contamination.

Hygiene

6-94. Personal hygiene should be of concern to leaders and Soldiers. Poor hygiene can lead to sickness and degradation of performance with an adverse effect on the unit as well as the Soldier. Cold temperatures found in mountain environments tend to aggravate hygiene issues. Often Soldiers neglect personal hygiene and field sanitation in cold weather. Food and water needs often take precedence over personal hygiene. Because of the extremes in temperatures and lack of bathing and sanitary facilities, keeping the body clean in a cold weather environment is not an easy proposition. Still, Soldiers need to attend to hygiene in the cold weather environment. (See FM 4-25.12 and FM 21-10 for a more robust sanitation technique listing.)

6-95. In cold weather mountain operations, Soldiers should shave daily and not allow hair to grow too long. A beard and longer hair adds little insulation and soils clothing with natural hair oils. In winter, a beard or a mustache becomes a nuisance since it serves as a base for the build-up of ice from moisture in the breath and can mask the presence of frostbite. Shaving daily is necessary but using a blade and soap removes protective face oils. Soldiers should shave several hours before exposure to the elements to reduce the danger of frostbite. This is usually done at the beginning of the rest cycle. Shaving with an electric razor does not remove the protective oils.

6-96. Soldiers should wash their entire body weekly (at a minimum). If bathing facilities are not available, Soldiers can wash with two canteen cups of water, using half for soap and washing and half for rinsing. Soldiers should clean feet, crotch, and armpits daily. They should also clean their teeth daily. It is important that Soldiers do not use alcohol-based wipes (commonly known as baby wipes) in the field. These wipes contain alcohol that conforms to the same temperature as the ambient air. If Soldiers use these products in an environment where the temperature is below freezing, then they risk contact frostbite, especially if the temperature is below 0 °F. Soldiers should change socks once per day at a minimum. If this is not possible, they should remove boots and socks and then dry and massage feet once per day.

6-97. Field sanitation and hygiene practices should include procedures for—
- Garbage.
- Latrines.
- Waste management.

EFFECTS ON EQUIPMENT

6-98. Some equipment may not function, or functions marginally, at high altitudes. On the average, vehicles lose 20 to 25 percent of their rated carrying capability and use up to 75 percent more fuel. Military generators and vehicles are often diesel-powered, but standard diesel engines lose efficiency at 3050 meters (10,000 feet) and eventually stop functioning altogether because of insufficient oxygen. Lubricants freeze; altitude and weather limit helicopters; and additional animal or gasoline-fueled overland transport adds to the physical demands and logistic requirements of this environment. Weapons also should be protected from environmental effects to include snow and ice. All personnel should know the problems associated with their particular equipment at high altitudes and take corrective action to ensure they function properly when needed. (For cold weather impacts on specific types of equipment and weapon systems, see FM 31-70.)

Infantry Weapons and Munitions

6-99. The functioning and employment of Infantry weapons is greatly affected by extreme cold temperatures. To properly handle and care for your weapons under a variety of adverse conditions, Soldiers should take the temperature, altitude, and precipitation into account. Weapons should be worked every thirty minutes to keep them from freezing. This should include racking the bolt, dropping the magazine, and pushing the ammunition to ensure they are not frozen together. Soldiers should become accustomed to manipulating their weapons in cold weather conditions while wearing bulky hand wear. Variables affecting weapon performance in cold climates include—
- Lubricants. Normal lubricants thicken causing stoppage or sluggish action. Use LAW (NSN 9150-00-292-9689) to lube weapons in colder temperatures (refer to individual weapons TM). Note that powdered graphite is not good for automatic weapons. Types of lubricants include the following:
    - Miltec lubrication.
    - Lubricant oil, semifluid, automatic weapons, temperate (LSAT). Use on MK-19.
- Condensation. This occurs when cold weapons are brought into a heated area (called sweating); it can continue up to an hour. Although it is worse from below to above freezing, sweating can still be caused by a large temperature change above freezing. Troop compartments in aircraft and vehicles should be kept cool. Body heat and breath can also affect optics under certain conditions.
- Breakage and malfunctions. Cold makes metal and plastic brittle. Melting snow and ice on weapons may cause stoppages (linked ammunition, tops of magazines, barrel and sights). Breakage also occurs during rapid warming of metal. Soldiers should initially fire at a slower rate, if possible.

- Visibility in ice fog. When water vapor in the air is crystallized, it forms fog. This occurs when temperatures are 20 degrees below zero and humidity is high. Fog can mask the line of sight. Soldiers should fire the weapon at a slower rate or relocate.
- Emplacement. If the terrain is hard, there is no shock absorption causing weapons breakage. If the terrain is soft, it gives under recoil of the weapon and the weapon must be adjusted. In slippery locations, the weapon may slide.

RESUPPLY CONSIDERATIONS

6-100. A variety of transport means are often required for logistical support. Road transport is often the most reliable and cost-effective. At higher altitudes where vehicles cannot be used due to climate and terrain conditions, pack animals may be used for transport of heavy logistical items. Sleds, mules, and horses in addition to vehicles, when possible, are a common site for mountain movement of supplies. When the conditions get too rough for even the animals, Soldiers must rely on themselves, local personnel, and air delivered supplies for logistical support. Due to the increased complexity and difficulty in its delivery to a final destination, logistical resupply items are generally pushed as far forward as possible when operating in mountain environments. Mountain weather and terrain slow and complicate all actions including resupply of ammunition and sustainment items. Supplies are often stored at a forward base in prepared packages of anticipated unit needs.

6-101. Logistics estimates and loads should be planned and customized for the mountain environment, specific locations, and unique conditions. For example, using pack animals requires that loads be broken up according to their carrying capacity. Overages should be built into supply estimates because there is usually a need for a large reserve of items that wear out quickly, such as boots, jackets, and gloves.

6-102. The road network in the mountains is generally a logistician's nightmare. Main supply routes to many areas are generally limited and often do not support vehicles that have a large turning radius. Roads often do not permit two-way traffic. While tactical plans take into account main roads, tactical engagements often occur away from these routes.

Movement of supplies

6-103. Movement of supplies for mountain operations is accomplished using one of four means. These include movement by air, vehicle, foot, or animal. Logistical movements down to the end user usually include a combination of movement types. For example, vehicles may transport supplies as far as possible into the mountains and then be carried by foot or animal to its final destination. Helicopters can transport supplies to remote, hard to reach locations but can be constrained by altitude and harsh weather. Since air assets are limited in number, in high demand, and cannot be used in extreme adverse weather, a mixture of resources is necessary to ensure reliability and flexibility. Porters are local personnel capable of carrying heavy loads across difficult terrain and may be contracted for use. The following means of transportation may be considered for use in mountain environments.

Foot

6-104. The preferred method of transportation of supplies is by any means other than on the backs of Soldiers. Even so, METT-TC conditions often dictate that Soldiers carry all the supplies needed for a particular mission. Litters may be used to help move supplies and equipment while traveling on foot. A litter can help Soldiers move heavier items (such as mortar rounds) through difficult areas and rough terrain. They can also be used in conjunction with ropes and pulleys to haul supplies up or down steep slopes.

6-105. Contract local personnel may also be available to assist in carrying supplies by foot. If available, these personnel can be used to carry excess supplies up to a particular point and then released. Supplies can also be stored in a cache for later use.

Vehicle

6-106. An analysis of mission needs versus transport time, cost, and asset availability, often makes movement by vehicle the preferred method of transport. Vehicles may include military vehicles as well as non-standard tactical vehicles, trucks, cars, four-wheel drive all terrain vehicles (ATVs), motorcycles, or other motorized means of transportation. Contract host nation vehicles may also be used for ground transportation movement of supplies in the mountains.

6-107. Resupply vehicle convoys are often the target of enemy ambushes. Unprotected convoys can fall into the hands of the enemy not only depriving friendly forces of the items and straining the logistical system, but also assisting the enemy with compromised ammunition or supplies.

Air

6-108. Movement of supplies by air is often the preferred method for remote, hard to reach locations when assets are available and the weather, terrain, and situation allow. Direct communication between the unit and the air delivery asset should be allowed and coordinated to help ensure proper delivery. An air drop of supplies in mountain terrain can quickly and easily turn into a resupply nightmare if not well coordinated. Supplies dropped to an area near the actual designated location can mean the difference between an easy, difficult, or a non-recovery of the supplies. Delivered packages can easily slide down a mountainside, slip off into a deep ravine, or disappear into deep snow if not placed properly. It is often difficult for pilots to identify and place packages at a precise location in the mountains if they are not in direct communication with the receiving unit. Supplies transported by aircraft are often configured by unit SOP and the actual drop off of packages from the aircraft accomplished in a variety of ways.

6-109. Air delivery systems are extensively used for resupply in mountain terrain. Deliveries to larger units may be conducted using containerized delivery systems dropped from higher altitudes using parachutes for lowering the supplies. For small-unit operations, air delivered supplies are packaged in smaller bundles and delivered through a variety of methods. Delivery platforms may be U. S. aircraft or the aircraft of other nations. Contract aircraft from host nation or other sources are also used for delivery of supplies. Leaders need to keep in mind that direct communication with host nation aircraft may be difficult or impossible and delivery procedures may not always be what the receiving unit is expecting. While a number of air delivery methods may be used, some of the most common methods used in mountain environments follow.

Unit Configured Loads

6-110. Unit configured loads (commonly known as "speedballs") are preconfigured resupply loads which may be delivered by helicopters. Supplies are often prepackaged in aviation kit bags, duffle bags, or other suitable containers by sustainment personnel for a quick response. Body bags, or "human remains bags", may be used to move supplies. These bags should be clearly marked with the word "SUPPLIES" stenciled in a bright color on the bag to avoid confusion. These bags are readily available through supply channels and have proven to be extremely useful because they are durable, waterproof, have carrying handles, can hold a large number of items, and can be folded and carried in a rucksack.

6-111. Helicopters pick up unit configured loads, fly as close to a drop off point as possible, reduce speed, drop supplies, and leave the area quickly to reduce exposure time. Supplies should be prepackaged in bubble wrap or other shock-absorbing material to minimize damage. This technique works well in the mountains, especially where there is a minimal or no air defense threat. Drop off locations should be marked if possible keeping in mind the risk of exposing the receiving unit's location. VS17 panels are commonly used for these purposes. In mountain conflicts, unit configured loads have become the delivery method of choice for delivery of supplies to remote unit locations hampered by distance and terrain. Unit locations such as a combat outpost on a mountain hilltop or ridge use these deliveries on a routine basis.

Sling Load and Rope

6-112. Sling load and rope deliveries are similar to unit configured loads except the supplies are lowered by rope or slung under the aircraft. Supplies and properly rigged equipment can be attached to a rope using a snap link and slid down. Once the supplies are received, the same rope can be used to back haul cans, containers, or other items. Care should be taken to ensure that a counterweight remains at the end of the rope so that it does not flap into the wind and catch the helicopter rotors. Care should be taken with heavy items so they don't slide down the rope and damage other supplies. Multiple water cans and "speed balls" can be linked together by means of a sling rope with a snap link attached. To slow the rate of descent, a round turn can be applied to the snap link holding the supplies. The rope can also be belayed from the ground to help control the rate of descent. In sling load operations the packaged supplies are suspended under the aircraft and set on the ground from a hover. Conducting these types of resupplies requires training and coordination prior to execution. Aircrews and ground support personnel must have an understanding of the procedures that are to be used. Sling load coordination requires certification of loads and air assault trained individuals to conduct hook up and drop operations to avoid damaging the load or aircraft or injuring a member of the aircrew or support personnel.

Low-Cost Low-Altitude Delivery

6-113.   Some supplies may be delivered by means of low-cost low-altitude (LCLA) parachute deliveries. Often, but not necessarily, these type of supplies are limited to food such as meals ready to eat and water. There are a number of systems that may be employed for LCLA deliveries, some being more accurate than others. Inaccurate deliveries on the side of a mountain can create a situation that requires extensive time and manpower for recovery of the supplies. If terrain and METT-TC conditions allow, sling load or unit configured load deliveries are often preferred. LCLA is performed by certified and trained aircrews, and is coordinated prior to execution to ensure minimal damage or loss.

Joint Precision Airdrop System

6-114.   If available, modern high-tech systems such as the Joint Precision Airdrop System (JPADS) may be used. The JPADS is a joint Army and Air Force aerial delivered package system dropped with a ram-air parachute and guided by a GPS. The GPS and steerable parachute works with the onboard computer to steer loads to a designated point on a drop zone. These systems can deliver supplies from over 15,000 feet and have them land inside a 100 foot circle of a designated location. These precision airdrops enable units in austere locations to receive supplies while keeping the aircraft safe at a high altitude. In the mountains, where air delivery is used extensively to re-supply forces in remote locations, large drop zones may be severely restricted by terrain and weather conditions. Use of JPADS does not require a large drop zone and could effectively save time and energy in retrieval of air delivered supplies.

Pack Animal

6-115.   Pack animals may be used for transportation of supplies. The use of pack animals (donkeys, mules, horses, and other animals) to aid in the movement of supplies and equipment is a standard practice in many mountain environments. Local personnel understand these animals' abilities, limitations, and most of all, how to load and control them. They also are skilled at providing the proper motivation to make the animals perform the required tasks. For planning purposes, the total load animals can carry normally does not exceed 25% of its weight. With practice heavy weapons such as the M2 and tube launched, optically-tracked, wire guide can be moved by pack animal.

6-116.   For example, a mule can carry up to 200 lbs. of cargo and traverse slopes up to 60 degrees. Panniers (baskets used on pack animals) can be rigged to carry just about anything, including weapons and ammo. Carts may also be used. A team of mules requires little maintenance and, if natural grazing material is available, mules need only graze 4 hours a day. If unavailable or inaccessible, mules can pack in their own grain and water.

6-117.   In planning for the use of pack animals leaders should consider the following questions:

- Is the terrain conducive to pack animal operations?
- Does altitude prohibit or restrict pack animal operations?
- Does seasonal bad weather prohibit or restrict pack animal use?
- Does the unit have experience navigating pack animals in limited visibility conditions?
- Does the unit have the training and experience to successfully execute pack animal operations?

- Are pack animals available for training and rehearsals?
- What types of pack animals are available in the operational area?
- What special equipment is required to conduct pack animal operations?
- What is the anticipated duration of the operation?
- Are there areas for the animal to graze or forage?
- Does the unit have the means to infiltrate the required equipment into the AO?
- Does the equipment require special rigging? Does it have special handling and storage requirements?
- Is the unit going to use the local pack equipment? Does the unit know about local pack equipment?
- Does the unit need to hire a local handler to pack the animals? Will the handler travel far from home?
- Is time available for the unit to plan and rehearse pack animal use before mission execution?
- Will time be available on the ground for the unit to rehearse packing the animals?
- Will there be time to acquire local equipment and feed, and to inspect animals if needed?
- Will unit have access to Veterinary Services?

6-118.   Although these animals can carry heavier loads for longer periods than Soldiers, they do tire. They should be cared for, fed, and watered. Their carrying capacity also decreases with higher elevations. Table 6-2 lists advantages and disadvantages of using pack animals.

Table 6-2. Pack animal considerations

Pack Animal Considerations	
Advantages	**Disadvantages**
May save energy and wear on troops.	Have terrain limitations, especially on narrow trails where wide loads limit their mobility.
May save time.	May have difficulty seeing during night movement with poor illumination.
Can carry larger loads than troops.	Must have proper feed (grain and roughage to sustain performance).
Payment for animals may stimulate the local economy in a counter-insurgency (COIN) situation.	May be difficult to secure and specifically targeted by the enemy.
Are readily available and replaceable if lost due to injury or combat action.	May be difficult to control and usually require a local handler.
Can carry crew-served and heavy weapons when properly secured and controlled.	Must have frequent water for sustained operations.
Offer leaders additional options in planning and execution.	May create operational security (OPSEC) concerns during coordination for use and planning.

Mission Sustainment

6-119.   Resupply to units conducting mountain operations can be a challenge. Resupply by military vehicles may be improbable or impossible and necessitate the use of other transportation means. Use of ATVs such as Gators may be possible in areas where other vehicles cannot travel if they are available. Vehicles may carry resupply items a far as possible and then be moved further by another means of transportation.

6-120.   Leaders should consider the distance and difficulty of terrain movements during travel to and from a resupply point if travel by foot is required. Crossing mountain terrain is often physically demanding to the point that Soldiers could exhaust themselves just by picking up supplies. Resupply efforts alone could leave

Soldiers less effective for their intended mission. Time and physical demands on the Soldiers often make dismounted retrieval from a distant drop off location a poor option.

6-121. More often, resupply to units in the mountains is conducted by some sort of air delivery. Due to the fact that suitable and safe LZs for aircraft in the mountains are hard to find, a common resupply delivery is accomplished by helicopters flying at a low altitude above the mountain terrain using unit configured load deliveries.

Caches

6-122. Caches may be used as a means of resupply to small units operating in mountain environments. There are two major concerns when considering the use of caches in the mountains. Of primary concern is the means to initially get the supplies to the point where they are to be stored for some period. Transportation of supplies to the site and its subsequent security are main considerations.

6-123. Caches are often used for dismounted patrols out for extended periods. These patrols often operate in areas where vehicular traffic is not possible. Supplies must be brought in by foot, animal, or air. Care should be taken to carefully store caches without disclosing their location. Even a properly concealed cache may be discovered by enemy personnel, aiding them and hindering the unit's mission.

Excess Supplies

6-124. Commanders should consider procedures for dealing with excess supplies during mountain operations. For supplies delivered by air to remote locations, pick-up or transportation of excess supplies is often impractical. Units that request specific types and amounts of supplies may be delivered more than what they need or can effectively use due to push system projections or other factors. Supply personnel often prepackage supplies in loads most often needed by size unit or in loads that would accommodate different types of units if requested. Regardless of the reason for the excess, these supplies cannot be left unattended and available for enemy personnel to find and use. Excess supplies that cannot be guarded, used, or picked up by friendly force personnel are commonly burned or otherwise destroyed according to unit SOP or commander's guidance.

CASUALTY/MEDICAL EVACUATION

6-125. CASEVAC or MEDEVAC operations in mountain terrain involve many challenges. Steep terrain and adverse weather are two main factors complicating evacuation. Even relatively minor injuries can lead to serious complications at high altitudes requiring evacuation. Air evacuation is often preferred but the weather, tactical situation, and other factors may preclude its use. Evacuations may be vertical as well as horizontal requiring units and personnel to be self sufficient in mountain evacuation techniques. A number of specialized techniques include methods for carrying sick and wounded personnel, and techniques for using ropes, manufactured litters, and rescue systems. Personnel should be familiar with how to package a patient for transport using the available systems.

6-126. During mission planning, leaders should outline procedures for casualty evacuations. Key considerations include—

- Planning extrication points along the route keeping in mind the unforgiving terrain.
- Carrying at least one or two compact and lightweight casualty transport systems.
- Coordinating for air assets and ground vehicles on stand-by for assistance in transportation.
- Ensuring a medic accompanies all patrols.
- Carrying VS-17 panels or other marking materials including night marking devices.
- Carrying additional combat lifesaver bags in addition to the medic bags.
- Carrying minimal mountain mobility equipment such as rope and carabineers.
- Rehearsing nonstandard platform CASEVAC.
- Rehearsing aerial MEDEVAC HOIST hookup and operations with aircraft personnel.

6-127. Air evacuation remains the preferred method for transporting sick and injured personnel. Due to the dispersed nature of troops, movement assets may take some time to arrive and expert medical help might not be readily available. Self-aid, buddy help, and combat life savers often provide medical assistance until casualties can be evacuated for higher level treatment. Medical support in the mountains is complicated by a number of factors including—

- The distances to medical facilities where advanced care must be given.
- Small mobile units in independent or semi-independent combat operations in remote areas.
- Slow or impossible ground evacuation.
- Altitude, terrain, and weather restrictions that hinder or delay aerial evacuation.
- Vulnerability of ground evacuation routes to enemy ambush.

6-128. There are several considerations to help overcome mountain evacuation complications. Some considerations include—

- Establishing aid stations with treatment and holding capacities at the lowest possible echelon. Patients evacuated by ground transport may be held until movement by secure means is possible. Use forward-stationed surgical teams for area medical support.
- Providing sufficient air or ground transportation to move medical elements rapidly.
- Establishing or reinforcing existing treatment and holding installations where there are numerous patients.
- Maximizing use of air evacuation, casualty evacuation, and medical evacuation, to include both scheduled and on-call evacuation support of static installations and combat elements in the field.
- Providing small medical elements to augment extended combat patrols.
- Considering assigning specially trained enlisted medical specialists to battalion casualty collection points for stabilizing treatment prior to the patients entering the brigade's evacuation chain.
- Strictly supervising sanitation measures, maintenance of individual medical equipment (both personal aid items and combat lifesaver kits/vehicle kits), and advanced first-aid training (combat lifesavers or equivalent) throughout the command.
- Increasing emphasis on basic combat training of medical service personnel, arming medical service personnel, and using armored carriers for ground evacuation where feasible.
- Establishing medical clinics at base locations. This affords trauma-level treatment to stabilize wounded until medical evacuation can occur. Additionally, clinics can serve to assist the local populace in areas where there is no medical support or affordable care.

6-129. If evacuation is necessary using either CASEVAC or MEDEVAC, the mission should be thoroughly coordinated and executed. Consider the following during mission execution for the evacuation.

- Ensure scene safety and security of personnel and patient. Scan the area for danger from mountain hazards as well as the enemy small arms fire and explosive devices.
- Ensure personnel do not become casualties themselves.
- Ensure medical personnel attend to patient.
- Protect the patient from the environment.
- Cause no further harm to the patient.
- Plan evacuation routes (smoothest route possible).
- Package patients for transport. Litters may be—
  - Improvised from rope, clothing, blankets, and other items.
  - Without poles.
  - Flexible and rigid collapsible casualty transport litters.
  - Air lifted for casualty transport litters.
  - Stokes basket.
- Ensure casualty report submission to unit S-1.
- Ensure completion of DA Form 1156, Casualty Feeder Card.

VEHICLE RECOVERY

6-130.   Harsh road conditions, harsh weather, and high altitudes have adverse effects on vehicles. Rough mountain roads can cause frequent vehicle breakdowns. High altitudes can reduce fuel efficiency and affect engine operation. If available, mechanics should accompany every mounted patrol into the mountains. If not available, personnel who work on broken down vehicles should be identified and carry the necessary tools. Recovery resources should be part of every mounted patrol and part of the pre-combat inspection, including tow straps, tow bars, winches, sand bags, and shovels.

6-131.   Vehicle recovery in mountain terrain can be extremely difficult. Steep terrain, narrow roads, and weather conditions can create an environment where recovery is complicated, time consuming, or impossible. When vehicles become disabled in mountain terrain, recovery alternatives include attempting to fix the vehicle with a contact team, towing it to a vehicle collection point, extracting it by heavy lift aviation assets, or destroying it in place. Recovery and on site repair by forward contact teams is preferred if possible.

6-132.   Units should also be capable of employing self-recovery techniques for instances where wreckers are not available or are prevented from deploying to the disabled vehicle site. Light-weight tow bars are useful but need to be used properly or they may become a liability. A minimum of two tow bars should be carried with every movement using vehicles. Vehicles with winches are also essential. Caution should be used when using chains and cables as they can easily break loose and allow the disabled vehicle to slide. Vehicle recovery plans should be rehearsed and each Soldier should know his part in vehicle recovery operations. Tactical, techniques and procedures found to be useful should also be shared between vehicles and units. Units should have a plan for moving disabled vehicles to clear a road or path.

OTHER ASSETS AND ATTACHMENTS

6-133.   Other assets that may be available or attached to an Infantry company operating in mountain environments include, but are not limited to, special teams, UAS, engineers, military working dogs (MWDs), and interpreters.

SPECIAL TEAMS

6-134.   Special teams may be identified by the company commander or platoon leader to perform specific tasks when required. Select platoons, squads, or fire teams are often identified as being responsible for these tasks and may be responsible for multiple tasks. Leaders attempt to maintain platoon, squad, and fire team integrity to the maximum extent possible when identifying special teams. Identification of special teams is a leader's responsibility and he may choose to designate as many or as few teams as he deems necessary. Common special teams are often identified in unit tactical SOPs but may be augmented with other teams depending on the environment and specific operation being conducted. Commanders organize their units for combat with consideration of teams needed for a specific mission. Common teams include—

- Aid and litter teams.
- Enemy Prisoner of War/Detainee teams.
- Surveillance teams.
- Assault teams.
- Support teams.
- Breech teams.
- Demolition teams.
- Site exploitation teams.

6-135.   Operations in mountain environments often create unique circumstances where designation of other special teams is common. Commanders may consider identifying additional teams to include—

- Rope installation teams.
- Cave and tunnel exploitation teams.
- Route reconnaissance teams.
- Landing zone teams.

6-136. During planning, preparation, organizing the company for combat, and designating special teams, the commander should consider the specific skill capabilities of individual Soldiers. Certain teams designated by the commander require that some Soldiers be knowledgeable on specific skills in order to perform unique functions. Operations in mountain terrain often require the use of these skills and the formation of teams from Soldiers that possess those abilities. The following list includes the three common levels of military mountaineering and their supporting skill sets.

Level 1: Basic Mountaineer

6-137. The basic mountaineer, a graduate of the basic mountaineering course, should be trained in the fundamental travel and climbing skills necessary to move safely and efficiently in mountainous terrain. Soldiers should be comfortable functioning in this environment and, under the supervision of qualified mountain leaders or assault climbers, can assist in the rigging and use of all basic rope installations. On technically difficult terrain, the basic mountaineer should be capable of performing duties as the "follower" or "second" on a roped climbing team, and should be well trained in using all basic rope systems. They may provide limited assistance to personnel unskilled in mountaineering techniques. Particularly adept Soldiers may be selected as members of special-purpose teams led and supervised by mountain leaders or advanced mountaineers. At a minimum, basic mountaineers should possess the mountain specific knowledge and skills listed below:

- Characteristics of the mountain environment (summer and winter).
- Mountaineering safety.
- Use, care, and packing of individual cold weather clothing and equipment.
- Care and use of basic mountaineering equipment.
- Mountain bivouac techniques.
- Mountain communications.
- Mountain travel and walking techniques.
- Hazard recognition and route selection.
- Mountain navigation.
- Basic medical evacuation.
- Rope management and knots.
- Natural anchors.
- Familiarization with artificial anchors.
- Belay and rappel techniques.
- Use of fixed ropes (lines).
- Rock climbing fundamentals.
- Rope bridges and lowering systems.
- Individual movement on snow and ice.
- Mountain stream crossings (to include water survival techniques).
- First aid for mountain illnesses and injuries.

NOTE: Level 1 qualified personnel should be identified and prepared to serve as assistant instructors to train unqualified personnel in basic mountaineering skills. All high-risk training must be conducted under the supervision of qualified level 2 or 3 personnel.

Level 2: Advanced Mountaineer (Assault Climber)

6-138.   Advanced mountaineers, or assault climbers, are responsible for the rigging, inspection, use, and operation of all basic rope systems. They are trained in additional rope management skills, knot tying, belay and rappel techniques, as well as using specialized mountaineering equipment. Advanced mountaineers are capable of rigging complex, multipoint anchors and high-angle raising/lowering systems. Level 2 qualification is required to supervise all high-risk training associated with Level 1. At a minimum, advanced mountaineers should possess the additional knowledge and skills listed below:

- Using specialized mountaineering equipment.
- Performing multipitch climbing on rock, leading on class 4 and 5 terrain.
- Conducting multipitch rappelling.
- Establishing and operating hauling systems.
- Establishing fixed ropes with or without intermediate anchors.
- Moving on moderate angle snow and ice.
- Establishing evacuation systems and perform high angle rescue.

Level 3: Mountain Leader

6-139.   Mountain leaders possess all the skills of the advanced mountaineer and have extensive practical experience in a variety of mountain environments in both winter and summer conditions. Level 3 mountaineers should have well developed hazard evaluation and safe route finding skills over all types of mountainous terrain. Mountain leaders are best qualified to advise commanders on all aspects of mountain operations, particularly the preparation and leadership required to move units over technically difficult, hazardous, or exposed terrain. The mountain leader is the highest level of qualification and is the principle trainer for conducting mountain operations. Level 2 qualification is required to supervise all high-risk training associated with Level 2. Instructor experience at a military mountain warfare training center or as a member of a Special Operations Forces (SOF) mountain team is critical to acquiring Level 3 qualification.

> Note: Army Special Operations Forces Mountaineering Operations Training Task in USASOC Regulation 350-12 states level 1 as being highest in the USASOC. The levels of training are essentially reversed. This is provided so readers understand that the USASOC levels are reversed compared to conventional units.

6-140.   At a minimum, mountain leaders should possess the additional knowledge and skills listed below:

- Preparing route, movement, bivouac, and operational risk management/ (Army) composite risk management.
- Recognizing and evaluating peculiar terrain, weather, and hazards.
- Performing avalanche hazard evaluation and mitigation.
- Organizing and lead avalanche rescue operations.
- Planning and supervising roped-movement techniques on steep snow and ice.
- Conducting glacier travel and crevasse rescue.
- Conducting ski instruction.
- Planning and conducting ski borne patrols in class 3 and 4 terrain.
- Using winter shelters and survival techniques.
- Conducting multipitch climbing on mixed terrain (rock, snow, and ice).
- Leading units over technically difficult, hazardous or exposed terrain in both winter and summer conditions.
- Advising commanders and staff during planning on mountain warfare considerations across all warfighting functions.

6-141. Table 6-3 depicts where Soldiers may obtain specialized mountaineering and cold weather operations skills. Levels correlate to the three common levels of military mountaineering training along with "S" for supporting which includes specialized training for certain MOSs or a unique skill.

Table 6-3. Military mountaineering and cold weather skill sources

COURSE NAME	LOCATION	DURATION	LEVEL
Basic Mountaineer Summer	Northern Warfare Training Center	15 days	1
Basic Mountaineer, Summer	Army Mountain Warfare School	14 days	1
Assault Climber	Northern Warfare Training Center	15 days (+ BM)	2
Assault Climber, Summer (Pre-req is Basic Mountaineer Summer)	Army Mountain Warfare School	14 days (+ BMS)	2
Basic Mountaineer, Winter	Army Mountain Warfare School	14 days	1
Assault Climber, Winter (Pre-req is Basic Mountaineer Winter)	Army Mountain Warfare School	14 days (+ BMW)	2
Cold Weather Orientation	Northern Warfare Training Center	4 days	1
Cold Weather Leaders	Northern Warfare Training Center	13 days	S
SF Senior Mountaineering	10th Special Forces Group Instructor Cadre	6 weeks	2
SF Master Mountaineering	10th Special Forces Group Instructor Cadre	3 weeks	3

UNMANNED AIRCRAFT SYSTEMS

6-142. The use of UAS, like all types of aircraft in the mountains, is dependent upon weather. Rain, fog, snow, wind, and other weather-related issues may preclude the use of UAS for an operation. When feasible, a UAS, such as the Raven, can be a valuable reconnaissance and security asset. UAS can be used to monitor and track movement in areas of key interest. An unmanned aircraft is not a completely stealth platform and can be spotted or detected by the hum of the engine by the enemy. They are also prone to interference from jamming devices.

6-143. UAS are often used in mountain operations—

- To gain knowledge on known or suspected enemy locations.
- To conduct reconnaissance on an area for a future planned operation.
- To observe or monitor otherwise unobservable areas (such as defilade, cracks, crevices and other concealed areas).
- To help provide security for a position.
- To cause enemy radio communications for COMINT purposes.
- To support security for combat outposts, raids, and patrols.
- For deception purposes.

6-144. A company level UAS, the RAVEN, can be employed at the commander's discretion. Commanders should determine if the advantages of using the system warrants employment for a particular operation. In the event helicopters are operating in the area, ground forces must alert them to the current location and altitude of tactically operated UAS. Coordination and communication from the company leadership to battalion ensure aircrews are alerted to airspace restrictions as they arise for UAS use. In mountain terrain where weather conditions can vary abruptly and easily crash a UAS, leaders may decide that risk of loss is too great to warrant their employment. Depending on unit SOPs, downed systems may have to be recovered. Recovering a downed unmanned aircraft in the mountains can be a slow and arduous operation and expose the recovery team to enemy actions.

6-145. Higher level UAS may be available for company and below operations but should be coordinated well in advance. Often these systems are used for preplanned operations rather than opportunity type missions and most often require a 72- to 96-hour pre-coordination.

MILITARY WORKING DOGS

6-146. Military working dog teams consist of one dog and one handler trained and certified as an entity. An Army MWD handler is usually a military police, combat engineer, or Special Operations Force Soldier, qualified in his or her primary military occupational specialty. The supported tactical commander, through consultation with the kennel master, should select the single purpose, or multi-purpose canine that best supports the mission. MWD capabilities include dogs specialized in one or more of the following areas:

- Patrol dogs provide a psychological deterrent, are a force multiplier, and are a show of additional force. This dog works primarily on-leash but can be worked off-leash, if needed. In either case, the patrol dog works close to his handler. All MWDs with "patrol" in their name are trained to bite and hold, with or without command. They are trained to detect people, not narcotics or explosives.
- Patrol narcotic detector dogs or patrol drug detection dogs are trained to recognize the scent of certain illegal substances and drugs through a program of practice and reward. The dog gives a response to trained odors and works on-leash.
- Patrol explosive detector dogs are useful in many searches or investigations involving explosives. This dog is used to detect explosives based on his response to the presence of trained odors. They work on- or off-leash.
- Mine detection dogs are trained to perform military mine-detection missions in a hostile environment. Their handlers are exclusively engineer Soldiers, and the mine detection dogs work on short lead or long line.
- Specialized search dogs are used in all types of area searches. They are trained to detect explosives, weapons, and ammunition. They work primarily off-leash. The handler, who may be a military police, engineer, or special operations Soldier, controls his specialized search dog using a multitude of command methods. These signals may be electronic, visual, and audible only to the dog.

INTERPRETERS

6-147. Interpreters are extensively employed and extremely beneficial while operating in mountain environments in foreign areas. Interpreters are often foreign personnel that also speak English as opposed to English speaking personnel that have learned the foreign language. This can present a number of issues. Leaders need to consider that when an interpreter is assigned to a unit, his foreign dialect may not be appropriate for the area in which they are operating. The interpreters conduct should be monitored for inappropriate behavior while interacting among the local population. Interpreters can be corrupt and use their position for monetary gain for themselves. Their actions may put the unit at risk as opposed to assisting them.

6-148. It is important that the interpreter understands they are there only to interpret and nothing else. Some interpreters may attempt to inappropriately add or take away some things said in order not to offend local personnel. It needs to be clear that their job is to translate precisely what is said. The level of English spoken by interpreters varies and the lack of a complete understanding of the English language can also create a problem. As with personnel in most organizations, some interpreters are better qualified than others.

6-149. Interpreters are usually at the ranking leader's disposal. They are there to assist and should be treated with the same respect as unit Soldiers. Leaders often have some things to teach to their interpreter as well as things they can learn from the interpreter about their culture. Using interpreters requires a two-way relationship with care and respect. It is important that all unit personnel remember that the interpreter can understand any comment or remark made by Soldiers. Any off-handed remark or small-minded insult can not only undermine the relationship with the unit but also potentially impact their combat mission.

HOST NATION FORCE AUGMENTATION

6-150. Host nation forces have the advantage of being in their homeland where they know more about the country, the situation, the terrain, and the culture than our own forces. They are a valuable resource for understanding the terrain in a particular area and can help save time and energy while planning and conducting operations. Host nation forces often have robust human intelligence capabilities since they know the terrain, local populace, and customs much better than U.S. forces and can often spot something that doesn't look right easier than U.S. personnel. Leaders should understand host nation force capabilities and limitations and use them accordingly.

6-151. Leaders should consider combined force operations from the augmenting force leader's perspective in order to better operate alongside them. Key points for leaders to consider should include—

* Including host nation leadership personnel in the planning stage of operations. They need to feel a part of the operation rather than a pawn in another commander's scheme. If these personnel are left out of planning they may be less willing to perform up to their full potential.
* Including host nation forces in rehearsals, pre-combat inspections, and pre-combat checks.
* Attaching U.S. advisors to host nation force leadership and embedded trainers, if available, to ensure the augmenting force understands and is prepared for missions. Leaders should consider that host nation units and personnel may not have the same standards or discipline as U.S. forces and may not perform in the same manner as expected of a U.S. Soldier.
* Providing U.S. forces for logistical support to host nation forces.
* Employing host nation forces within their capabilities. They often do not have the same capabilities as U.S. Soldiers and units.
* Intermingling host nation forces with their own unit while conducting missions such as combat patrols. Host nation personnel often look to the U.S. Soldier for actions and guidance during conflicts.
* Establishing effective relationships with host nation forces based on a personnel rapport built by key leaders.
* Using host nation forces to help in searching operations while on patrols. U.S. Forces may be restricted on entering dwellings while host nation forces can often enter houses with fewer limitations and search restricted areas.

6-152. Host nation forces are often collocated with U.S. forces in an established position such as an operating base. These forces should be integrated into the overall defensive plan for the base and may be given a portion of the perimeter to defend with their fires integrated with the U.S. unit. Leaders from both forces need to understand the importance of integrating the units for a combined defense. Contingency plans should be established for failure of the host nation portion of the defensive perimeter.

Glossary

Acronym	Definition
A	
ACTK	assault climber team kit
AMS	acute mountain sickness
AO	area of operations
ATV	all terrrain vehicle
B	
BCT	brigade combat team
C	
C2	command and control
CAS	close air support
CASEVAC	casualty evacuation
CBRN	chemical, biological, radiological, and nuclear
CCA	close combat attack
CCM	close combat missiles
COIST	company intelligence support teams
COMINT	communications intelligence
CP	command post
G	
GPS	global positioning system
H	
HACE	high altitude cerebral edema
HAMK	high angle mountaineering kit
HAPE	high altitude pulmonary edema
I	
IED	improvised explosive device
IPB	Intelligence Preparation of the Battlefield
ITAS	Improved Target Acquisition System
J	
JPADS	joint precision airdrop system
JTAC	joint terminal attack controller
L	
LCLA	low cost low altitude
LOS	line of sight
LRAS3	long range advanced surveillance system
LZ	landing zone

M

MEDEVAC	medical evacuation
MET	meteorological
METT-TC	mission, enemy, terrain, weather, troops, and support available, time available, and civil considerations
MG	machine gun
MTC	movement to contact
MWD	military working dog

N

NCO	noncommissioned officer

O

OP	observation post

P

P.A.C.E.	primary, alternate, contingency and emergency
PMESII-PT	political, military, economic, social, information and infrastructure, with the addition of physical environment and time

R

RETRANS	retransmission

S

SIMK	snow and ice mobility kit
SLM	shoulder launched munitions
SOP	standard operating procedure

T

TACSAT	tactical satellite
TLP	troop leading procedures

U

UAS	unmanned aircraft systems

V

VHF	very high frequency

W

WP	white phosphorus

References

SOURCES USED
These are the sources quoted or paraphrased in this publication.

ATTP 3-18.12, *Air Assault Operations,* 1 March 2011.

FM 1-02, *Operational Terms and Graphics,* 21 September 2004.

FM 2-01.3, *Intelligence Preparation of the Battlefield/Battlespace,* 15 October 2009.

FM 3-0, *Operations,* 27 February 2008.

FM 3-04.203, *Fundamentals of Flight,* 7 May 2007.

FM 3-09.32 *(JFIRE) Multiservice Tactics, Techniques, and Procedures for the Joint Application of Firepower,* 20 December 2007.

FM 3-21.8, *The Infantry Rifle Platoon and Squad,* 28 March 2007.

FM 3-21.10, *The Infantry Rifle Company,* 27 July 2006.

FM 3-21.20, *The Infantry Battalion,* 13 December 2006.

FM 3-22.10, *Sniper Training and Operations,* 19 October 2009.

FM 3-34.170, *Engineer Reconnaissance,* 25 March 2008.

FM 3-36, *Electronic Warfare in Operations,* 25 February 2009.

FM 3-90, *Tactics,* 4 July 2001.

FM 3-97.6, *Mountain Operations,* 28 November 2000.

FM 3-97.61, *Military Mountaineering,* 26 August 2002.

FM 4-25.11, *First Aid,* 23 December 2002.

FM 4-25.12, *Unit Field Sanitation Team,* 25 January 2002.

FM 5-0, *The Operations Process,* 26 March 2010.

FM 5-19, *Composite Risk Management,* 21 August 2006.

FM 21-10, *Field Hygiene and Sanitation,* 21 June 2000.

FM 31-70, *Basic Cold Weather Manual,* 12 April 1968.

FM 90-4, *Air Assault Operations,* 16 March 1987.

TB MED 505, *Altitude Acclimatization and Illness Management,* 30 September 2010.

TB MED 507, *Heat Stress Control and Heat Casualty Management,* 3 July 2003.

TB MED 508, *Prevention and Management of Cold Weather Injuries,* 4 January 2005.

TC 2-19.63, *Company Intelligence Support Team,* 9 November 2010.

USARAK Pamphlet 385-4, *Risk Management Guide for Cold Weather Operations,* 30 September 2009.

REFERENCED FORMS
DA Forms are available on the APD web site (www.apd.army.mil).

DA Form 1156, Casualty Feeder Card.

DA Form 2028, Recommended Changes to Publications and Blank Forms.

ORGANIZATIONAL RESOURCES
These organizations can provide additional information.

Army Mountain Warfare School   https://www.benning.army.mil/amws/

Northern Warfare Training Center http://www.wainwright.army.mil/nwtc/

Asymmetrical Warfare Group http://www.awg.army.mil/

PEO Soldier https://peosoldier.army.mil/

USMC Mountain Warfare Training Center http://www.mwtc.usmc.mil/

WEBSITES

Army Knowledge Online, https://akocomm.us.army.mil/usapa/doctrine/index.html

Reimer Doctrine and Training Digital Library, http://www.train.army.mil

Army Publishing Directorate, http://www.apd.army.mil/

Index

By Order of the Secretary of the Army:

GEORGE W. CASEY, JR.
General, United States Army
Chief of Staff

Official:

JOYCE E. MORROW
Administrative Assistant to the
Secretary of the Army
1103805

DISTRIBUTION:

Active Army, Army National Guard, and U.S. Army Reserve: To be distributed in accordance with
the initial distribution number (IDN) 116013, requirements for ATTP 3-21.50.

www.ingramcontent.com/pod-product-compliance
Lightning Source LLC
Chambersburg PA
CBHW080207300326
41934CB00038B/3394